Allen v. Allen

Second Edition

Deposition File
Faculty Materials

Allen v. Allen

Second Edition

Deposition File
Faculty Materials

Andrew I. Schepard
Siben & Siben Distinguished Professor of Family Law
Hofstra University
Maurice A. Deane School of Law

Gregory Firestone, PhD
Affiliate Associate Professor
University of South Florida
College of Public Health
President, Global Resolutions LLC (aka *My Florida Mediator*)

Philip M. Stahl, PhD, ABPP (Forensic)
Private Practice

Sonya Johnson, CPA, ABV/CFF
Girard & Johnson, LLC
(Financial Forensic/CPA Services)

NITA®
National Institute for Trial Advocacy

Address inquiries to:

Reprint Permission
National Institute for Trial Advocacy
1685 38th Street, Suite 200
Boulder, CO 80301-2735
Phone: (800) 225-6482
Fax: (720) 890-7069
Email: permissions@nita.org

ISBN 978-1-60156-819-9
eISBN 978-1-60156-820-5

FBA 1819

Printed in the United States of America

SUSTAINABLE FORESTRY INITIATIVE
Certified Chain of Custody
Promoting Sustainable Forestry
www.sfiprogram.org
SFI-01347

Wolters Kluwer

Official co-publisher of NITA.
WKLegaledu.com/NITA

Dedication

This edition of the case file is dedicated to Louis Ortiz, our colleague, friend, and co-author on the first edition, who recently passed away. He was a wonderful and kind man and an extremely talented CPA and financial expert. More important, his genuine courtesy to others always made the sometimes contentious litigation process more positive. We miss him.

Contents

ACKNOWLEDGEMENTS

The authors acknowledge the contributions of the following to this edition of the *Allen* case file:

Arline S. Rotman, a now retired, model family court judge and a co-author on the first edition of the case file who helped bring it to life.

Anita M. Ventrelli, Stacy Preston Collins, Tracy Farryl Katz, and Tina Fujisaki, who adapted an earlier version of the *Allen* case file for use in the joint ABA Family Law Section (ABA-FLS)–National Institute for Trial Advocacy (NITA) Annual Family Law Trial Advocacy and allowed us to use their materials, particularly the trial exhibits, in this edition.

Mark Caldwell, NITA's Resource Director, who facilitated the agreement to allow use of the ABA-FLS–NITA materials in this edition.

Kate Haggerty of Powerplays Coaching LLC, a gifted actor, who has played Lynne Allen often and provided us with valuable insights about how to shape the characters for this edition.

Marsi Buckmelter, our intrepid editor from NITA Publications, who supported us, guided us, and appropriately nagged us to finish this project.

And to the generations of law, mental health and accounting students, and professionals who used the earlier editions of the *Allen* file in their courses and continuing education programs and whose comments helped make it better.

The National Institute for Trial Advocacy wishes to thank Facebook for its permission to use likenesses of its website as part of these teaching materials.

INTRODUCTION

This file is intended for use for depositions in the divorce case of *Allen v. Allen* focusing on the following disputed issues:

- what parenting plan is in the best interests of the Allen children; and
- what is the value of the accounts receivable of David Allen's radiological practice for purposes of equitable distribution.

The file is organized so that depositions in the parenting dispute can be taken separately from depositions in the valuation dispute, though they can be taken together in a single program on deposition skills.

Witnesses to be deposed on parenting issues are David Allen, Lynne Allen, and a court-appointed, neutral expert psychologist. Witnesses to be deposed in the valuation dispute are two experts, one for each side, on the valuation of the accounts receivable. Various exhibits are also available for use at the depositions. Mental health and valuation consulting expert reports for each side are also provided to help plan depositions.

This NITA case file uses a dating system that begins with YR-0 as the current year and progresses back in time with YR-1 as the current year minus one year, YR-2 as the current year minus two years, and so forth. For example, the date which the Allens married is YR-15 which is fifteen years ago from today. Jane was born on February 2, YR-13, and thus was born thirteen years ago. If it is 2019, the date of her birth would be February 2, 2006. Please refer to the dates by this system.

An electronic version of all exhibits are available for download at http://bit.ly/1P20Jea; the password is Allen2.

Time Line

May YR-17	David Allen graduates from medical school.
June YR-16	David Allen and Lynne Grant meet while David is a resident and Lynne is working at the same hospital as a patient representative.
February 2, YR-15	David Allen and Lynne Grant marry.
June YR-14	David Allen finishes his residency.
September YR-14	David Allen establishes solo radiology practice.
February 2, YR-13	The Allens' first child, Jane, is born.
April 17, YR-11	The Allens' second child, Joey, is born.
November YR-10	The Allens leave their Nita City apartment to move to the suburbs.
September YR-6	Lynne resumes her education at Nita University.
June YR-4	Lynne earns a BA in communications and starts work at a radio station, WKJW, for a salary of $30,000 per year.
September YR-3	Lynne accepts a full-time position as assistant programming director at WKJW.
November YR-3	David begins an affair with his x-ray technician, Norma Starks.
January YR-2	During an argument, David tells Lynne about his affair with Norma.
Late January YR-2	David moves out of the house for a month and stays with Norma and her children.
February YR-2	Lynne creates and makes a sales pitch for a successful radio show, *Baseball Widows*, with syndication possibility.
Late February YR-2	David Allen returns to the marital residence.
May YR-2	Lynne begins affair with James Porter.
February YR-1	Lynne kicks off *Baseball Widows* during spring training.
March YR-1	David Allen's Petition for divorce filed and served.
May YR-1	Lynne Allen's Answer and Counterpetition for divorce filed.
May YR-1	David Allen and Lynne Allen establish a parenting schedule by agreement in which David has overnights with Jane and Joey every other weekend and on Wednesday evenings.
January YR-0	Court order for parenting evaluation entered.

Court Files

IN THE SUPERIOR COURT OF
DARROW COUNTY, STATE OF NITA
FAMILY DIVISION

David Allen, Petitioner	)))	
v.	)	Docket No. 1954-A
Lynne Allen, Respondent	)))	

PETITION FOR DISSOLUTION OF MARRIAGE

1. Petitioner, who resides at 437 Elm Street, Huntington, Nita, 09997, was lawfully married to Respondent, who now resides at 437 Elm Street, Huntington, Nita 09997.
2. The parties were married at Nita City, Nita, on February 2, YR-15, and last lived together at 437 Elm Street, Huntington, Nita, and still reside together.
3. The minor children born of this marriage are Jane Allen, born February 2, YR-13, and Joey Allen, born April 17, YR-11.
4. Petitioner certifies that no previous action for divorce, annulling, or affirming marriage; separate support; desertion; living apart for justifiable cause; or residence of the minor children has been brought by either party against the other with no exceptions.
5. On or about January 5, YR-2, the marriage suffered an irretrievable breakdown.
6. Wherefore, Petitioner requests that the Court:
   a. Grant a divorce for irretrievable breakdown;
   b. Prohibit Respondent from imposing any restraint on Petitioner's personal liberty;
   c. Grant Petitioner parenting responsibility for the above-named children;
   d. Order a suitable amount for support of minor children;
   e. Order conveyance to Petitioner of the real estate located at 437 Elm Street, Huntington, Nita, standing in the names of Lynne Allen and David Allen as recorded with the Huntington County Registry of Deeds, Book 5370, Page 28;

f. Order an equitable division of all assets;

g. Grant such other relief as the Court deems appropriate and just.

Respectfully submitted,

TINKERS, EVERS & CHANCE

By:

Frank B. Chance

Frank B. Chance

Attorney for Petitioner
411 Main Street
Nita City, Nita 09999
(555) 555-3000

Dated: March 21, YR-1

IN THE SUPERIOR COURT OF
DARROW COUNTY, STATE OF NITA
FAMILY DIVISION

David Allen, Petitioner	)))	
v.	)	Docket No. 1954-A
Lynne Allen, Respondent	)))	

ANSWER AND COUNTERPETITION OF RESPONDENT TO PETITION FOR DISSOLUTION OF MARRIAGE

Respondent Lynne Allen in the above-captioned matter and in response to Petitioner's Petition for Divorce dated March 21, YR-1, files this answer:

1. Respondent admits the allegations of Paragraph 1 of Petitioner's Petition.
2. Respondent admits the allegations of Paragraph 2 of Petitioner's Petition.
3. Respondent admits the allegations of Paragraph 3 of Petitioner's Petition.
4. Respondent admits the allegations of Paragraph 4 of Petitioner's Petition.
5. Respondent admits the allegations of Paragraph 5 of Petitioner's Petition.
6. Wherefore, in response to Petitioner's requests pursuant to Paragraph 6, Respondent respectfully requests that this Honorable Court:
   a. Grant Respondent parenting responsibility for the minor children of the marriage;
   b. Order a suitable amount of support for Respondent and for minor children;
   c. Order conveyance to Respondent of the real estate located at 437 Elm Street, Huntington, Nita, standing in the names of Lynne Allen and David Allen as recorded with the Huntington County Registry of Deeds, Book 5370, Page 28;
   d. Order an equitable division of all assets;

e. Allow Respondent to resume her former name of Lynne Grant;

f. Grant such other relief as the Court deems appropriate and just.

Respectfully submitted,

HERNANDEZ, CARTER & FETTERMAN

By:
Victoria Fetterman
Victoria Fetterman

Attorney for Respondent
Nita Bar Building, Suite 222
Nita City, Nita 09999
(555) 555-9000

Dated: May 4, YR-1

Parenting Plan Dispute Materials

MATERIALS AVAILABLE TO ALL COUNSEL

IN THE SUPERIOR COURT OF
DARROW COUNTY, STATE OF NITA
FAMILY DIVISION

David Allen, Petitioner	)))	
v.	)	Docket No. 1954-A
	)	
Lynne Allen, Respondent	))	

ORDER FOR PARENTING PLAN EVALUATION

At the last conference in this matter, the Court concluded that the best interests, rights, or wishes of the minor children, Jane, DOB February 2, YR-13, and Joey, DOB April 17, YR-11, require the appointment of a parenting plan evaluator.

At the Court's request, the parties have each recommended three psychologists to serve as parenting plan evaluator. After due consideration, under the authority of Nita Evidence Code § 730, the Court hereby orders:

1. Pat Nolan, PhD, recommended by counsel for the Petitioner, will serve as a parenting plan evaluator.
2. The parenting plan evaluator shall report back to the Court on issues regarding legal decision making for and residence of the minor children and any other matter related to what parenting plan is in the children's best interests.
3. The parenting plan evaluator shall have authority to do any and all of the following as the evaluator deems necessary and appropriate to prepare the report for the Court:
    a. To contact any or all people having relevant knowledge regarding any member of the family.
    b. To consult with any professional with specialized knowledge.
    c. To require psychological or medical evaluations of any and all family members and/or caretakers.
    d. The parties are to contact the evaluator and arrange to provide the evaluator with whatever information is necessary for each to carry out their functions.
4. The parties should arrange for themselves and the children to go to the evaluator's office and to attend to all appointments as requested by the evaluator. They shall also provide the evaluator with whatever documents requested.
    a. Parties shall submit all written materials to the evaluator and simultaneously submit materials to the other party's attorney. The evaluator shall not consider any written material not meeting this condition.

   b. If the evaluator desires, the parties are to make arrangements for the evaluator to see the conditions under which the children live.

5. The parties, or their attorneys, recognize that there is no confidentiality in the evaluation to the extent that the information in the evaluation is necessary for the Court to make a determination of a parenting plan that is in the best interests of the children.

6. The Court-approved *Notice Regarding Confidentiality of Child Custody Evaluation Report* must appear on the first page of the report when the evaluator files the report with the Clerk of the Court and serves it on the parties or their attorneys, and any counsel appointed for the child, to inform them of the confidential nature of the report and the potential consequences for the unwarranted disclosure of the report.

7. The evaluator's report, which shall be filed with the Court and served on counsel as soon as the evaluation is complete, shall contain:

   a. A description of the purpose of the evaluation.

   b. A description of any limitations in the evaluation that result from unobtainable information, failure of a party to cooperate, or the circumstances of particular interviews.

   c. Recommendations for decision-making and residence only for a party who has been evaluated. This requirement does not preclude the evaluator from making an interim recommendation that is in the best interests of the children.

   d. Clear, detailed recommendations that are consistent with the health, safety, welfare, and best interests of the children if making a recommendation to the Court regarding a parenting plan. The recommendations should make specific references to the factors listed in Nita Family Code § 61.058. Recommendations may include referrals to mediation, counseling, or therapy.

   e. A summary of the data-gathering procedures, information sources, and time spent, and present all relevant information, including information that does not support the conclusions reached. The summary shall also include a description of any limitations in the evaluation that result from unobtainable information, failure of a party to cooperate, or the circumstances of particular interviews.

   f. The data collection and analysis procedure used to gather data for the report shall allow the evaluator to observe and consider each party in comparable ways and to substantiate (from multiple sources when possible) interpretations and conclusions regarding each child's developmental needs; the quality of attachment to each parent and that parent's social environment; and reactions to the separation, divorce, or parental conflict. This process may include:

      i. Reviewing pertinent documents related to parenting plan, including local police records.

      ii. Observing parent-child interaction (unless contraindicated to protect the best interests of the children).

iii. Interviewing parents conjointly, individually, or both conjointly and individually (unless contraindicated in cases involving domestic violence), to assess:

a. capacity for setting age-appropriate limits and for understanding and responding to the child's needs;

b. history of involvement in caring for the child;

c. methods for working toward resolution of the conflict over a parenting plan;

d. history of child abuse, domestic violence, substance abuse, and psychiatric illness; and

e. psychological and social functioning.

iv. Conducting age-appropriate interviews and observation with the children, both parents, stepparents, step- and half-siblings conjointly, separately, or both conjointly and separately, unless contraindicated to protect the best interests of each child.

v. Collecting relevant corroborating information or documents as permitted by law.

vi. Consulting with other experts to develop information that is beyond the evaluator's scope of practice or area of expertise.

g. A description of the examiner's qualification to render the opinions in the report, including a list of all the publications authored in the previous ten years.

8. The evaluator's report is to be completed within ninety days of the entry of this order, and the evaluator shall distribute the report to the Court and counsel in a manner designed to ensure its receipt and to preserve its confidentiality.

9. Each party shall initially pay 50 percent of the costs of the evaluation and any deposition or trial testimony by the evaluator. The percentage paid by each party is subject to reallocation after trial of this action.

10. Any parent may depose the evaluator in advance of trial at a time and place mutually agreed upon by counsel and the parties.

It is ORDERED AND ADJUDGED.

DONE AND ORDERED in Chambers in Nita City, Nita, this 19th day of January, YR-0.

SUPERIOR COURT JUDGE

Copies: Both Parties
Counsel for the Parties
Dr. Pat Nolan

SUMMARY OF LEGAL RESEARCH

1. The Nita Rules of Civil Procedure are identical to the Federal Rules of Civil Procedure.
2. The Nita Rules of Evidence are identical to the Federal Rules of Evidence.
3. Nita is a "pure" no-fault divorce state. The only ground for divorce in Nita is "irreconcilable differences."
4. Nita Family Code § 61.058. Parenting of children following dissolution of marriage provides as follows:
   a. Parental responsibility means the relationship between the parents relating to decisions that must be made regarding the minor child and a time-sharing schedule for the parents and child. The issues concerning the minor child may include, but are not limited to, the child's education; health care; and physical, social, and emotional well-being. In creating a plan for parental responsibility, the court must take into account all circumstances between the parents, including their historic relationship, domestic violence, and other factors.
   b. Following dissolution of marriage, the court shall order that the parental responsibility for a minor child be shared by both parents unless the court finds that shared parental responsibility would be detrimental to the child. If the court determines that shared parental responsibility would be detrimental to the child, it may order sole parental responsibility and make such arrangements for visitation as will best protect the child or abused spouse from further harm. Regardless of whether there is a conviction of any offense of domestic violence or child abuse or the existence of an injunction for protection against domestic violence, the court shall consider evidence of domestic violence or child abuse as evidence of detriment to the child.
      i. In ordering shared parental responsibility, the court may consider the expressed desires of the parents and may grant to one party the ultimate responsibility over specific aspects of the child's welfare or may divide those responsibilities between the parties based on the best interests of the child. Areas of responsibility may include primary residence, education, medical and dental care, and any other responsibilities that the court finds unique to a particular family.
      ii. The court shall order sole parental responsibility, with or without visitation rights, to the other parent when it is in the best interests of the minor child.
   c. In determining parental responsibility and allocation of each parent's time with their children, the court's evaluation of the best interests of the child shall include an evaluation of all factors affecting the welfare and interests of the child, including, but not limited to:
      i. The parent who is more likely to allow the child's frequent and continuing contact with the other parent;

ii. The love, affection, and other emotional ties existing between the parents and the child;

iii. The capacity of the parent to provide the child with food, clothing, medical care, or other remedial care recognized or permitted under the laws of this state in lieu of medical care, and other material need;

iv. The length of time the child has lived in a stable, satisfactory environment and the desirability of maintaining continuity;

v. The permanence of the family unit, and of the existing proposed custodial home;

vi. The moral fitness of the parents;

vii. The mental and physical health of the parents;

viii. The home, school, and community record of the child;

ix. The history of interpersonal conflict, including any incidents of domestic violence;

x. Any other fact considered by the court to be relevant.

Stipulations for Parenting Plan Depositions

1. Both parents orally agreed without court order to the current temporary parenting plan. David has overnights with Jane and Joey every other weekend and on Wednesday evenings.
2. Neither party has sought an interim parenting order from the court.
3. All entries on the parenting plan evaluator's CV are accurate.
4. Neither party can seek discovery of the parenting plan evaluator's notes or work product, nor use the fact that none are available for any purpose at trial.
5. Both David's and Lynne's lawyers have each retained a consulting parenting plan expert to review and comment on the evaluator's report. Communications between each mental health consultant and the lawyer who retained the consultant are protected from disclosure by the attorney work product doctrine.
6. The Superior Court of Nita decided not to appoint a lawyer or guardian to represent Jane and Joey Allen in the parenting dispute.
7. The Superior Court of Nita decided not to interview Jane or Joey Allen as part of its fact-gathering process to determine the Allens's parenting dispute.
8. The parties have exchanged document requests. The exhibits to this case file were produced in discovery and available to both sides.

Exhibits

Exhibit 1

FROM THE DESK OF JOHN PAULSON

March 15, YR-0

Dear Dr. and Mrs. Allen:

I am writing to express my concerns about your children's emotional health. I have received reports from both children's teachers concerning an alarming change in the children's behavior. Other school personnel have given me similar reports. Both children are psychologically deteriorating at a rapid rate. It is vital that I meet with you immediately to discuss my concerns and possible remedies.

Please call me to discuss this matter. My direct line is (555) 966-4213, or you can email me at Paulson.J@nitadistrict31.nita. Thank you.

John Paulson, PhD
Psychologist
Nita District 31

Exhibit 2

HUNTINGTON COMBINED SCHOOLS
96 HOWLAND ROAD
HUNTINGTON, NITA 09999
(555) 720-2496 MAIN
(555) 720-2497 FAX

March 20, YR-0

Dr. and Mrs. David Allen
437 Elm Street
Huntington, Nita 09997

RE: Jane's academic progress, attendance, and attitude

Dear Dr. and Mrs. Allen:

I write to express the concern of Jane's academic team. You will note from her attached third-quarter report that she has substantially stumbled this academic term. Her grades have slipped, sometimes dramatically; her efforts in doing work are less than ever before, her attitude is no longer positive; and she is missing or tardy from class far above school standards. Frankly, we are worried.

I would like to schedule a time when the two of you can meet with Jane's team, including Dr. Paulson, the District 31 psychologist, to discuss the changes in Jane's behavior, attitude, and performance. Please contact the school secretary, Mrs. Evelyn Sandusky, at (555) 720-2496 at your earliest convenience to schedule an after-school appointment.

I know Jane and she is just not acting herself these days. Here at Huntington, we want to do everything to ensure Jane's success as a student and member of our school community. I look forward to hearing from you and our mutually developing a plan to help Jane regain her academic footing.

Sincerely,

Fredrick Robinson, PhD
Academic Dean

Attachment

Exhibit 3

Name: Jane Allen **Grade:** 08

Dr. & Mrs. David Allen
437 Elm Street
Huntington, Nita

The Mission of the Huntington Combined School is to provide excellence in education through a nurturing environment where students can develop the knowledge, skills, and values for continuous learning.

HUNTINGTON COMBINED SCHOOLS
96 Howland Road, Huntington Nita
YR - 0 Academic Year

A = Excellent
B = Above Average
C = Average
D = Experiencing Difficulty
F = Failing

P = Pass
I = Incomplete

Conduct & Effort
1 = Excellent
2 = Good
3 = Fair
4 = Poor

	Term 1	Term 2	Term 3	Term 4
Absences	0	0	8	
Tardies	0	0	15	

61 Read 2B	1st	2nd	3rd	4th	FNL
• Conduct • Effort	A 1 1	A 1 1	C 4 3		
A pleasure as a student. I am worried about decrease in effort and conduct					

61 Math 2D	1st	2nd	3rd	4th	FNL
• Conduct • Effort	B 1 1	B 1 1	C 3 2		
A big change in attitude and effort this quarter. Is something going on at home?					

61 Soc 2D	1st	2nd	3rd	4th	FNL
• Conduct • Effort	B 1 1	B+ 1 1	C - 4 4		
Poor attitude in class. Missed many assignments					

Art 6	1st	2nd	3rd	4th	FNL
• Conduct • Effort	B 1 1	B 1 1	C 2 2		
Missing assignments					

Spanish 6	1st	2nd	3rd	4th	FNL
• Conduct • Effort	B - 2 2	B - 2 2	C + 3 3		
Shows little interest in class. Socializes too much					

61 Eng 2C	1st	2nd	3rd	4th	FNL
• Conduct • Effort	B+ 2 2	A 1 1	C 3 4		
A drop off in effort and conduct. It is like Jane no longer cares about her work.					

61 Sci 2A	1st	2nd	3rd	4th	FNL
• Conduct • Effort	A 1 1	A 1 1	B- 3 3		
Failure to turn in assignments resulted in grade change					

61 Choir 6	1st	2nd	3rd	4th	FNL
• Conduct • Effort	P 1 1	P 1 2	P 2 2		
A pleasure as a student. Jane missed a concert!					

Comp Sci 6	1st	2nd	3rd	4th	FNL
• Conduct • Effort	A - 1 1	B + 2 2	C + 2 3		
Jane is showing less interest in class and her assignments					

Phys Ed 6	1st	2nd	3rd	4th	FNL
• Conduct • Effort	A 1 1	A 1 1	B + 2 2		
Jane is doing great with her gymnastics. I see she is a lot of weight. Is this planned?					

Team 61 Homeroom 109

Grade Point Average				
1st	2nd	3rd	4th	FNL
3.44	3.38	2.22		

I have read the following report: ______________________ ______________

Parent or Guardian Signature Date

Exhibit 4

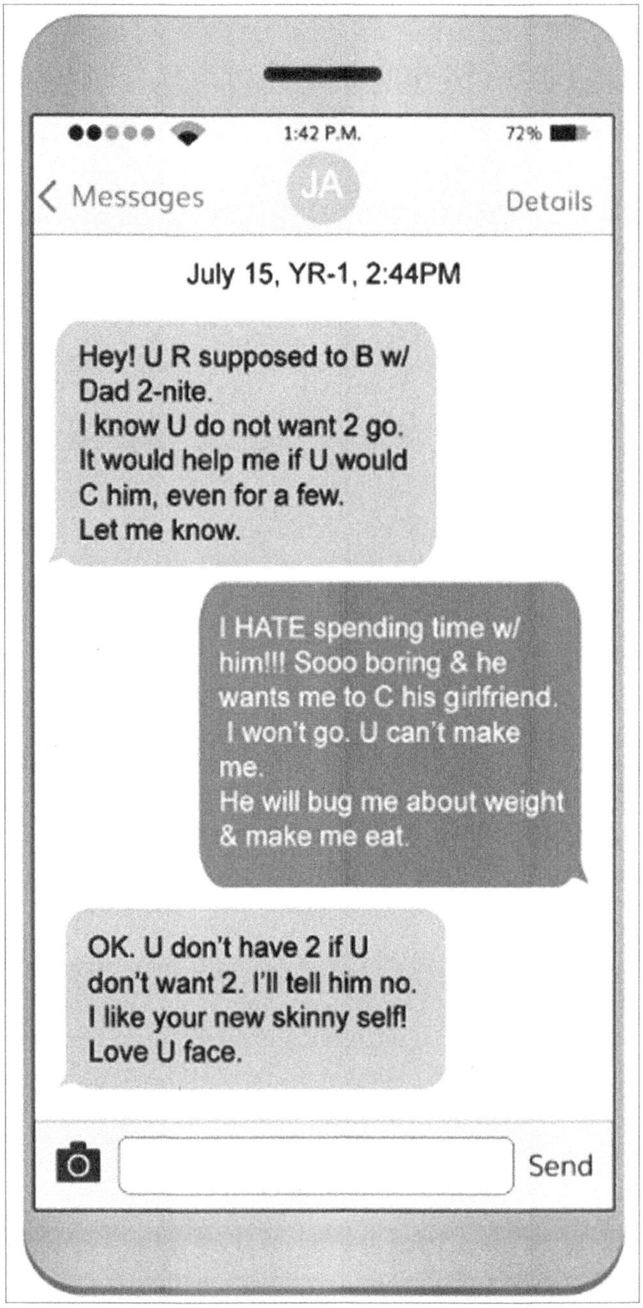
1:42 P.M.
72%
Messages
JA
Details
July 15, YR-1, 2:44PM
Hey! U R supposed to B w/ Dad 2-nite. I know U do not want 2 go. It would help me if U would C him, even for a few. Let me know.
I HATE spending time w/ him!!! Sooo boring & he wants me to C his girlfriend. I won't go. U can't make me. He will bug me about weight & make me eat.
OK. U don't have 2 if U don't want 2. I'll tell him no. I like your new skinny self! Love U face.
Send

FROM: Lynne Allen <speak2lynne@geemail.nita>
DATE: Monday, September 15, YR-3, at 3:05 PM
TO: David Allen <drdavid@powerdiagnostics.nita>
SUBJECT: I need you to watch the kids tonight

I have a business dinner I need to attend tonight. You need to watch Jane and Joey for me. Please be home in time for when they get home from school.

Lynne

Lynne Allen
Assistant Programing Director
WKJW
(555) 953-6802
speak2lynne@geemail.nita
Are you listening to Baseball Widows – the hottest sports show for women?

FROM: David Allen <drdavid@powerdiagnostics.nita>
DATE: Monday, September 15, YR-3, at 3:10 PM
TO: Lynne Allen <speak2lynne@geemail.nita>
SUBJECT: RE: I need you to watch the kids tonight

You've got to be kidding me! You aren't the only one who is busy. I'll get John to cover for me for my last appointments. What time do I need to be home?

Why couldn't you schedule this meeting for earlier in the day?

David

Important Notice to Recipients

Please do not use email to request prescription refills or to convey medical information. We cannot execute such instructions provided by email. HIPAA prohibits sharing medical information via email.

The sender of this message is an employee of Power Diagnostics Radiology Practice. If you have received this communication in error, please destroy all electronic and paper copies and notify the sender immediately. Erroneous transmission is not intended to waive confidentiality or privilege.

FROM: Lynne Allen <speak2lynne@geemail.nita>
DATE: Mon, Sept 15, YR-3, at 3:30 PM
TO: David Allen <drdavid@powerdiagnostics.nita>
SUBJECT: RE: I need you to watch the kids tonight

This just came up. It is an important meeting with a big-time producer who is interested in syndicating my show. If you support my career, you will do this for me.

Jane has gymnastics this afternoon and will be home around 5:00. She is getting a ride from one of the other mothers. Joey will be home around 4:00.

We've talked about this before. My career is important to me, and this is my big opportunity.

Lynne

Lynne Allen
Assistant Programing Director
WKJW
(555) 953-6802
speak2lynne@geemail.nita
Are you listening to Baseball Widows – the hottest sports show for women?

FROM: David Allen <drdavid@powerdiagnostics.nita>
DATE: Monday, September 15, YR-3, at 3:35 PM
TO: Lynne Allen <speak2lynne@geemail.nita>
SUBJECT: RE: I need you to watch the kids tonight

John has agreed to take my last couple of appointments. I am on my way now.

Please don't make this a habit. This is the third time you've met with this guy for dinner. My schedule is just as busy as yours.

Try not to come home smelling of alcohol. It's a bad impression for the kids.

David

Important Notice to Recipients

Please do not use email to request prescription refills or to convey medical information. We cannot execute such instructions provided by email. HIPAA prohibits sharing medical information via email.

The sender of this message is an employee of Power Diagnostics Radiology Practice. If you have received this communication in error, please destroy all electronic and paper copies and notify the sender immediately. Erroneous transmission is not intended to waive confidentiality or privilege.

FROM: Lynne Allen <speak2lynne@geemail.nita>
DATE: Monday, September 15, YR-3, at 3:38 PM
TO: David Allen <drdavid@powerdiagnostics.nita>
SUBJECT: RE: I need you to watch the kids tonight

You are a dear!

Please don't be so prudish. Having a couple of drinks over a business dinner is expected and part of my business.

I will be home around 10:00.

Lynne

Lynne Allen
Assistant Programing Director
WKJW
(555) 953-6802
speak2lynne@geemail.nita
Are you listening to Baseball Widows – the hottest sports show for women?

Exhibit 6

FROM: David Allen <drdavid@powerdiagnostics.nita>
DATE: Wednesday, September 17, YR-1, at 3:10 PM
TO: Lynne Allen <speak2lynne@geemail.nita>
SUBJECT: This weekend

Lynne:

Norma's son Jim is in the state baseball championship game this Saturday in Rochester, Nita. I am taking Jim, Norma, and Kelly to the game, and we are making a family adventure of it. We will go to the Falls after the game is over for a sightseeing tour. Jim and Kelly want Jane and Joey to come with us for the weekend. We need to be there as a family to support Jim and have fun afterwards.

David

Important Notice to Recipients

Please do not use email to request prescription refills or to convey medical information. We cannot execute such instructions provided by email. HIPAA prohibits sharing medical information via email.

The sender of this message is an employee of Power Diagnostics Radiology Practice. If you have received this communication in error, please destroy all electronic and paper copies and notify the sender immediately. Erroneous transmission is not intended to waive confidentiality or privilege.

FROM: Lynne Allen <speak2lynne@geemail.nita>
DATE: Wednesday, September 17, YR-1, at 3:12 PM
TO: David Allen <drdavid@powerdiagnostics.nita>
SUBJECT: RE: This weekend

You have to be kidding. This is my weekend with Jane and Joey. We have activities planned, including a gymnastics practice for Jane and a party with friends for Joey. I don't understand how you didn't know about your own children's lives. Or you may not care. Norma and her children are not your family. Jane and Joey are.

Lynne

Lynne Allen
Assistant Programing Director
WKJW
(555) 953-6802
speak2lynne@geemail.nita
Are you listening to Baseball Widows – the hottest sports show for women?

Exhibit 7

Search for people, places and things
Home Find Friends
You Can Do It! You Can Survive Baseball Season!
Baseball Widows
Timeline About Photos Friends More
Photos
Baseball Widows
1hr
He might not want to quit his day job of singing.
clevver NEWS
Justin Bieber FALLS Skateboarding in NYC!
Like Comment Share Delete
Baseball Widows
February 15, YR-2, at 10:15am
Big news! We have started negotiations with several sports networks to put "Baseball Widows" into syndication. Things are looking good that we could go national by the start of next season. Talk about Hot Stove discussions, this could mean big things for the show and WKJW.
I will continue as hostess with the mostest! Some things will change as we expand our sports talk to more teams. The Nita Naturals will still be my favorite Minor League team, but we will shift to more talk about the big leagues. Of course, we will feature the Nats' parent organization, the Colorado Rockies, but the discussion will expand to more teams.
We will also be expanding to other sports as well, including professional and college football, basketball, and hockey. Look for a name change to "Sports Widows" as we go national.
Like Comment Share Delete
There are no more posts to show.
Facebook © YR-1 · English (US)

Exhibit 8

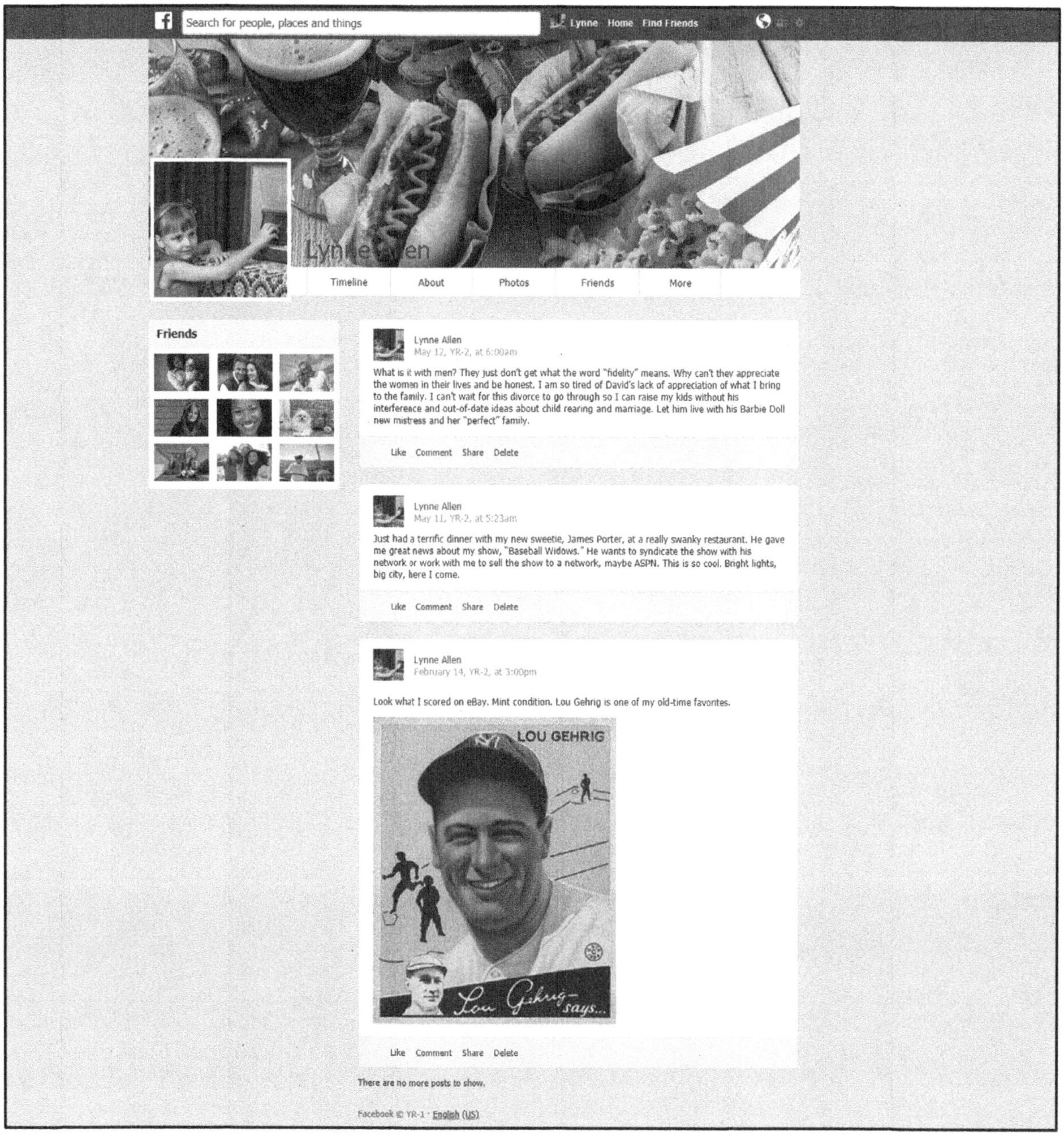

Search for people, places and things

Lynne Home Find Friends

Lynne Allen

Timeline About Photos Friends More

Friends

Lynne Allen
May 12, YR-2, at 6:00am

What is it with men? They just don't get what the word "fidelity" means. Why can't they appreciate the women in their lives and be honest. I am so tired of David's lack of appreciation of what I bring to the family. I can't wait for this divorce to go through so I can raise my kids without his interference and out-of-date ideas about child rearing and marriage. Let him live with his Barbie Doll new mistress and her "perfect" family.

Like Comment Share Delete

Lynne Allen
May 11, YR-2, at 5:23am

Just had a terrific dinner with my new sweetie, James Porter, at a really swanky restaurant. He gave me great news about my show, "Baseball Widows." He wants to syndicate the show with his network or work with me to sell the show to a network, maybe ASPN. This is so cool. Bright lights, big city, here I come.

Like Comment Share Delete

Lynne Allen
February 14, YR-2, at 3:00pm

Look what I scored on eBay. Mint condition. Lou Gehrig is one of my old-time favorites.

Like Comment Share Delete

There are no more posts to show.

Facebook © YR-1 · English (US)

Court-Appointed Parenting Evaluator Dr. Pat Nolan's Report and CV

FL-328 Notice Regarding Confidentiality of Child Custody Evaluation Report

(1) **Case name:** Allen v. Allen

(2) **Case number:** 03-12345

If directed by the court, the child custody evaluator must file a written, confidential report of his or her evaluation. At least 10 days before any hearing regarding custody of the child, the report must be filed with the clerk of the court and served on the parties or their attorneys and counsel appointed for the child.

Important Notice: This form must be attached as the first page of the child custody report. The child custody evaluation report MUST NOT become part of the public court file. It is confidential and private.

THE ENCLOSED CHILD CUSTODY EVALUATION REPORT IS CONFIDENTIAL

Unwarranted Disclosure of the Report

You must not make an unwarranted disclosure of the contents of the child custody evaluation report. A disclosure is unwarranted if it is done either recklessly or maliciously and is not in the best interest of the child.

- **Monetary Sanctions:** If the court determines that an unwarranted disclosure of a written confidential report has been made, the court may order a fine against the disclosing party in an amount that is large enough to prevent that person from disclosing information in the future.
- **Attorney Fees and Costs:** The sanction may also include reasonable attorney fees, costs incurred, or both, unless the court finds that the disclosing party acted with substantial justification or that other circumstances make the imposition of the sanction unjust.

Potential Consequences for the Unwarranted Disclosure of the Report

By law, the court can impose a penalty for the unwarranted disclosure of the child custody evaluation report. The penalty for the unwarranted disclosure of the child custody report can include monetary sanctions (a fine) and attorney fees and costs.

Access to the Report

This report may not be made available to anyone other than the following (Fam. Code, §§ 3025.5, 3111):

a. The parties and their attorneys (including attorneys from whom the parties seek legal representation) and attorneys appointed to represent the child

b. Court professionals who would receive it directly from the court to do their job, including:

- Family court judicial officers
- Family court employees
- Family law facilitators
- Juvenile court judicial officers
- Juvenile probation officers
- Child protective services workers
- Law enforcement officers
- Probate court judicial officers
- Guardianship investigators

c. Others, but only by court order

Confidential Report for Attorneys and the Family Court Only.

The enclosed report is not part of the public court file. It is confidential and private.

Authorized recipients of this report must not make an unwarranted disclosure of its contents. A disclosure is unwarranted if it is done either recklessly or maliciously and is not in the best interests of the child.

By law, the court can impose a penalty for unwarranted disclosure, which can include monetary sanctions (a fine) and attorney fees and costs.

Pat Nolan, PhD
777 Washington Blvd., Suite 225, Nita City, Nita 09999
V/M: (555) 555-5555 • Fax: (555) 555-6666
Email: pnolan@nitagreatshrink.nita

PARENTING EVALUATION

Name: Allen, David and Lynne

Dates of evaluation: February 9, 20, 23, 28; March 8, 14, 22, 29; April 6, 14, 22, 25, 30, YR-0

Evaluated by: Pat Nolan, PhD

Nita case no: 03-12345

REASON FOR REFERRAL

This evaluation was requested in order to assist in diagnostic understanding and aid in determination of a parenting plan for their minor children Jane, age 13 (DOB 2/2/YR-13) and Joey, age 11 (DOB 4/17/YR-11).

EVALUATION PROCEDURE

Complete written and verbal informed consent was obtained from Dr. and Ms. Allen before undertaking this court-ordered evaluation, and both parties signed necessary releases of confidentiality. The procedures for the evaluation were thoroughly discussed with the parents. Limits of confidentiality, specifically that there was no confidentiality within this evaluation process and with the attorneys and the court, were discussed with both parents, with the children, and with all relevant collateral witnesses.

This evaluation consisted of the following:

- Conjoint interviews, Dr. and Ms. Allen (each approximately one hour), February 9 and April 30, YR-0.
- Individual interviews, Dr. Allen (each approximately one-and-one-half hours), February 23, March 14, April 25, YR-0.
- Individual interviews, Ms. Allen (each approximately one-and-one-half hours), February 20, March 22, April 22/YR-0.

- Office interviews with the children (each approximately two hours), February 28, March 8, April 6, April 14, YR-0. Father brought the children on February 28 and April 6, and mother brought the children on March 8 and April 14. During the interview on February 28, the children were seen conjointly for thirty minutes and individually for forty-five minutes each. On March 8, the children were each seen individually for one hour. On April 6, the children were seen individually for thirty minutes each and one hour was spent conjointly with the children and their father. On April 14, the children were seen individually for thirty minutes each and one hour was spent conjointly with the children and their mother.
- Conjoint interview, Ms. Norma Starks and her children, Jim (age eleven) and Kelly (age nine) (approximately one hour), March 29, YR-0.
- Review of written materials supplied by Dr. and Ms. Allen and/or their attorneys. Since both sides were copied on all materials, a listing of materials is not included in this report.
- Brief conjoint phone calls with attorneys on January 27 and February 28.
- Collateral phone calls with:
  - Dr. Sturm, mother's therapist, March 12 (fifteen minutes)
  - Dr. Paulson, school psychologist, March 19 (fifteen minutes)
  - Dr. Henne, family pediatrician, March 20 (fifteen minutes)
- Letters on behalf of Dr. Allen were sent by Dr. Allen's father, and by friends and colleagues Jim Thornton, Mark Heller, and Ruth McVay.
- Letters on behalf of Ms. Allen were sent by Ms. Allen's mother, and by friends and colleagues John Marleau, Susan Ricci, and Jane Shanahan.

This evaluator will typically administer psychological testing when it is seen as relevant and helpful to the evaluation. Given that neither the parents nor their attorneys saw a reason for it and nothing suggesting a significant mental health problem was raised in either the interviews or the parents' depositions, no psychological testing was administered.

BRIEF BACKGROUND AND INFORMATION

According to information available to this examiner from both parents, this couple married in YR-15 and initially separated in YR-2. However, a month after Dr. Allen moved out of the marital home, he returned, and both parents have continued to live in the marital home, albeit with considerable tension.

History reveals that early on in their relationship, they got along reasonably well and continued to function well together when they moved from Nita City to the suburbs in YR-10 after the children were born. Tension developed when Ms. Allen went back to school in YR-6 and started working in YR-4. Once Ms. Allen started working, tension increased, as Dr. Allen believed she became much less supportive of him and his work, and she believed that Dr. Allen was unsupportive of her and her work.

Both parents acknowledge that each of them had previously been active parents. Dr. Allen had frequently taken the children on outings, supervised their homework, and generally participated in most aspects of parenting. As a doctor, he also took responsibility for the children's medical care. Before going to work at the radio station, Ms. Allen had engaged in many of the primary tasks of parenting, including cooking meals, feeding and bathing the children; putting them to bed; and getting up with them in the night. When Ms. Allen started working, Dr. Allen adjusted his schedule and became more involved with the day-to-day care of the children, spending more of his evenings with Jane and Joey and fewer with his journals. Meanwhile, Ms. Allen continued to devote a substantial amount of time and energy to caring for the children. She was insistent that they not be "shortchanged" by her return to work.

Tension continued as Ms. Allen spent even more time in her radio job. Her duties in programming were expanded, and she was given control of new feature developments. Dr. Allen felt that Ms. Allen was barely managing to have time for her work and the children and that she had no time for their relationship. By this point, Ms. Allen and Dr. Allen were barely communicating. Both parents reported that their previously active sex life deteriorated dramatically. On a number of occasions in late YR-3, Ms. Allen called on Dr. Allen at work, requesting that he take care of Jane and Joey so that she could work late at the station. More than once, this required Dr. Allen to leave his practice during busy periods to rush home to care for his children. Twice, Ms. Allen arrived home very late with alcohol on her breath. This alcohol use was a dramatic break from her past behavior.

By this time, Dr. Allen had begun an affair with his x-ray technician, Norma Starks. During one particularly heated argument in early January YR-2, Dr. Allen told Ms. Allen about his affair with Ms. Starks and announced he wanted a divorce so he could continue his involvement with Ms. Starks openly. After Dr. Allen admitted his affair to Ms. Allen, he left the marital residence and stayed with Ms. Starks in her apartment in the city. This continued for about a month, after which Dr. Allen moved back into the marital residence, where he currently lives with Ms. Allen and the children. Dr. Allen told Ms. Allen that he moved back in because he didn't want their marital difficulties to harm his relationship with the children, which he feared would be likely if he lived out of the house. Dr. Allen sleeps in the guest bedroom in the house, separate from Ms. Allen. Like many parents, they told the children very little about these changes, causing the children to feel increasingly anxious and insecure about what was going to happen.

About the same time, Ms. Allen presented the WKJW managing board with a new feature proposal for their 1:00 p.m. weekday slot. The time slot had been a thorn in the side of station management for some time, plagued by low ratings and declining advertising revenues. Ms. Allen proposed trying a sports program with a new angle. The show would be pitched to "baseball widows," women with husbands so obsessively involved with sports that the wives felt "widowed" during the season. The program would cover college and pro baseball, highlight current action, and provide background and education about the sport. All features would be constructed from a woman's perspective and in a slightly humorous vein. The station accepted the proposal and suggested that Ms. Allen host *Baseball Widows* herself. Ms. Allen felt that she understood the concept and possessed the requisite sports knowledge to pull it off. *Baseball Widows* had its broadcast debut as spring training commenced in YR-1. She is currently at the point of entering negotiations with several radio networks, which may be the major turning point in her radio career.

Within the context of these family changes, the couple cannot agree on a permanent parenting plan for the children. They have temporarily agreed that they will share joint legal and physical custody of the children, with the children and each parent remaining in the family home, and Dr. Allen having responsibilities for the children every Wednesday from after school overnight and every other weekend from Friday to Sunday and Ms. Allen being responsible for the children the rest of the time. However, Dr. Allen is not satisfied with the time-sharing arrangement and neither is satisfied that this will work once the parents physically separate, with each of them seeking primary physical custody of the children.

They find themselves arguing more often and more bitterly, and more often in front of the children. Dr. Allen has rejected Ms. Allen's suggestions that they go to counseling, saying that their relationship is over. Ms. Allen has put herself in individual therapy on a once a week basis with a psychologist (Dr. Sturm) whose office is near her office. Ms. Allen has told her husband that the focus of her therapy is an attempt to work out the tension she feels in balancing career concerns and family responsibilities. She has also periodically suggested that Dr. Allen move out again, but Dr. Allen has steadfastly refused. There is significant tension in the house. Dr. Allen and Ms. Allen sleep in separate bedrooms. Dr. Allen spends some evenings at Ms. Starks's apartment, but most nights he sleeps at home.

Dr. Allen and Ms. Allen have told their children they are having marital problems, and the children have overheard their frequent arguments. The children have been seriously affected by the strains in their parents' marriage. Despite their temporary agreement, Jane often refuses to participate in activities with her father, as she appears very angry at him. Dr. Allen blames Ms. Allen for this, but Ms. Allen says that Jane is angry at her father due to her perception that he spends more time and interest with his girlfriend Norma Starks and her family than with Jane and Joey.

Given their respective concerns about the children and their inability to manage their dispute, the parents and their attorneys stipulated to this court-ordered evaluation.

PARENTS' CONCERNS

Dr. David Allen

Dr. Allen presented as a friendly, cooperative man who related reasonably well with this examiner. As he talked, his affect was generally positive, especially when focusing on the children and his perception of their needs. He is concerned about the children and how each of them is adjusting to the family tension. By and large, he feels optimistic that things will work out. During the evaluation, he stayed focused on these issues, and there was no evidence of rambling or any significant psychopathology. His major concerns are that Ms. Allen does not agree to him having sufficient time with the children and interferes with his relationship with Jane.

As he talked about the issues, he admitted that he feels somewhat guilty about his affair with Ms. Starks, but he is also angry at and frustrated with Ms. Allen. He still has some affectionate feelings for her, but he believes that the marriage is over. He does not feel that marriage counseling is an option. He is concerned that his wife has changed drastically over the years, and he feels she abandoned him and the children for her career and that she is becoming neglectful of the children as her job demands increase. He thinks Ms. Starks will be a terrific mother to the children, whereas he believes that Ms. Allen currently is not. In discussing this with him, he indicated that he meant she would fill the mother role well, not that she is replacing Ms. Allen.

Dr. Allen indicated that he would like to marry Ms. Starks after the divorce is final. After they marry, Ms. Starks can devote a great deal of time and effort working on her relationship with Jane and Joey. Dr. Allen is unwilling to move out of the marital residence until the divorce and parenting issues are settled. He fears that if he moves out, he will not get back in. He also fears that moving out now will prejudice his claims to be the primary parent of the children. He is not happy about the tension that exists while he and Ms. Allen are living under the same roof, but he could not think of anything that he could do to improve the situation.

Dr. Allen wants to be the primary parent of both children because he feels that Ms. Allen is too involved in her emerging career and would have insufficient time and energy for the children. He added that his increased involvement with the children in the last few years has made him realize not only how important it is to be an involved father, but also that he can provide the care and guidance the children need to grow. He is willing to consider shared parenting, but he is upset about Ms. Allen's reaction to the children's present difficulties and feels this does not bode well for the future. He is also concerned that Ms. Allen is interfering in his relationship with his daughter and is trying to undermine the children having a relationship with Ms. Starks. He is very troubled by the "barriers" she erects to Ms. Starks's relationship with the children. He is particularly concerned about Ms. Allen's influence on Jane. Dr. Allen feels that Jane idolizes the person Ms. Allen has become, which he feels fosters a very negative image. Dr. Allen says that he is open to Ms. Allen spending a "reasonable" amount of time with the children if he becomes the primary parent of the children. Regardless of the parenting plan, he is adamantly opposed to any restrictions on the children's relationship with Ms. Starks, despite Jane allegedly being upset that Ms. Starks has asked the children to call her "Mom."

Dr. Allen is also very concerned about the emotional well-being of the children, especially Jane. Based on his own observations, the letter from the school psychologist, and the follow-up meeting with school personnel, he feels that a mental health evaluation of both children is called for and that therapy for both children is advisable. He has a colleague at Nita Medical Center who is a very well-qualified child psychologist whom he would like the children to see because he "is competent and will do it at a reduced rate." Ms. Allen has been reluctant to permit this, which makes him angry. Dr. Allen is willing to participate in family therapy (with Ms. Allen, Jane, and Joey) to facilitate the divorce and his and Ms. Starks' relationship with the children as well as to advance his goal to be the primary parent, provided the aim of the therapy is divorce adjustment, not reconciliation with Ms. Allen.

In general, Dr. Allen has been upset and angry at Ms. Allen for putting her own needs for a career above those of their marriage and family. He was unable to describe any way in which he is contributing to the marital problems.

Dr. Allen is also concerned that his wife is seeing another man. She often comes home very late in the evening with no explanation of where she has been. She often calls, texts, or emails Dr. Allen and asks him to take care of the children to work late at the station. Dr. Allen is suspicious of her late nights. He has never confronted her about it, nor has he seen her on a date with anyone else, but he believes that an affair is the only explanation for Ms. Allen's behavior.

When asked what the children need, he spoke about the children needing a relationship with Ms. Starks, largely because he expects to marry her, and she will be available for the children when he is at work. Of course, he also believes that the children need both him and his soon-to-be ex-wife involved with them. While he talked about some concerns about Joey's symptoms and Jane's weight issues, his primary feeling was that the children needed him to be the primary parent so they could get to know Ms. Starks better. He believes that "if they do not, Ms. Allen will not only undermine the children having a relationship with Ms. Starks but will use that bad relationship with Ms. Starks to undermine the relationship with me," which he states has already begun with Jane. He recognizes their need for a healthy relationship with both him and their mother. While he understands their need to adjust to the divorce, he also believes that he is better suited to meeting their medical needs. Upon inquiry, Dr. Allen indicated his belief that this means the children would be with their mother every other weekend and one dinner visit weekly, and all other time would be with him. He also indicated his desire to share holidays and breaks from school, allowing for reasonable vacations during breaks from school.

Dr. Allen was also asked about his plans after the divorce is final. Most of them are outlined above. In addition, he thinks it is important to keep the children in their current school district. He indicated, assuming that he did not remain in the marital home, he would get an apartment, initially without Ms. Starks, and he will only have Ms. Starks move in after the children have become more settled in their relationship(s) with her and are ready for a day-to-day relationship. It is likely that he will get another house when things are fully settled after the divorce is final and he and Ms. Starks are married.

Ms. Lynne Allen

Ms. Allen also presented as a friendly, cooperative woman who related reasonably well with this examiner. As she talked, her affect was generally positive, especially when focusing on the children and her perception of their needs. She is concerned about the children and how each of them is adjusting to the family tension. She is quick to blame Dr. Allen for most of these problems, and she is concerned that things will not work out easily for them. It was clear that she has strong feelings of anger and resentment toward Dr. Allen. She is very uncomfortable whenever she talks about those feelings, and she cried or spoke with intensity when talking about him. During the evaluation, she stayed focused on these issues. There was no evidence of rambling or any significant psychopathology.

From the beginning, Ms. Allen expressed outrage about Dr. Allen's adultery. She had considerable difficulty talking about Ms. Starks. She repeatedly voiced her fear that Dr. Allen is encouraging Ms. Starks to take her place with the children. While she is angry with him for the affair, she also opened up that she began a relationship with a successful radio executive shortly after she started working full time. The executive, James Porter, is forty-one years old, very attractive, and has never been married. Mr. Porter showed an immediate interest in Ms. Allen and in her budding career, just as Dr. Allen was growing increasingly resentful of her work. The affair started one night when they got together for dinner at a time when she was particularly angry with Dr. Allen. She has been seeing Mr. Porter regularly for dinner, drinks, etc., sometimes in Nita City, and sometimes in Huntington or the nearby area. For several of these encounters, Ms. Allen called on Dr. Allen to watch the children while she and Mr. Porter met. Although her husband has suspected her recent relationship, she hasn't told him or the children and she doesn't think that the children know about it. She likes Mr. Porter, but is unsure where the relationship is going. It could be a fling, but at the very least Mr. Porter seems very interested in Ms. Allen and her career. Ms. Allen was clear that Mr. Porter would like their relationship to become very serious. It is evident that while she is outraged by Dr. Allen's affair, she does not see how her own affair is problematic, largely because hers began around the time she and Dr. Allen separated

Despite her anger, when talking about the divorce, Ms. Allen spoke ambivalently. At times, she still loves Dr. Allen and feels that there is a possibility that the marriage could work. At other times, she talks like the marriage is over and does not want to stay married to Dr. Allen. She says she is trying hard to resolve her conflicted feelings in therapy but is having great difficulty in doing so. She feels that Dr. Allen is too selfish about having things go his way. She has been clear that her career is very important to her and that she doesn't want to stay married to a man who doesn't respect her desire to be a success. She has voluntarily been in therapy since Dr. Allen moved back into the house, as she is trying to gain insight into her own role in their marital problems. She says that the therapy hasn't yet helped her resolve her ambivalence about continuing the marriage or her anger at Dr. Allen and Ms. Starks.

Ms. Allen feels that Dr. Allen's infidelity coupled with his unreasonable rigidity about her need for a real career is responsible for their marital difficulties. She is angry with him and feels that he has forfeited any "rights" he might have by his behavior. If Dr. Allen is unwilling to give up Ms. Starks, Ms. Allen wants him to move out of the house and into his own apartment. She wants him to decide this quickly so that the shouting and the arguments will stop. She is worried about the effects these scenes are having on the children and on her. Ms. Allen is unwilling to move out herself.

Ms. Allen was clear that she wants to be the primary parent of the children and is adamantly opposed to sharing the residential parenting equally. She recognizes that Dr. Allen is a committed father and should play a role in the children's lives; however, she is concerned that if Dr. Allen and Ms. Starks marry, Joey and Jane will be taken away from her. She worries that Ms. Starks will become their mother and that she will be shut out. These insecurities may make it difficult for her to support the children's relationship with their father and his girlfriend. Ms. Allen believes that Ms. Starks will do anything she can to win Jane and Joey over and to supplant her. She speaks of Ms. Starks in harsh and bitter terms. She feels that if Dr. Allen gets equal parenting time with the children, he will use his power to help Ms. Starks supplant her in the children's lives. If she is granted the right to be the primary parent, she is "willing to give David reasonable parenting time, but only if the children want to see him." She doesn't want the children forced to see him if they don't want to. She also wants to limit Ms. Starks's influence over them, preferring that Ms. Starks not be around when their father sees them. She has little insight into how her behavior can be considered restrictive gatekeeping and how it can negatively impact the children's relationship with their father and his girlfriend.

Ms. Allen is very concerned about Jane's and Joey's reaction to the current marital stress. She is reluctant to have them examined by a mental health professional, especially one of Dr. Allen's choosing. She is afraid Dr. Allen will use this as an opportunity to influence the children to side with him in any dispute. Ms. Allen sees Jane's anger at Dr. Allen as being a natural reaction to his unacceptable conduct and has said that if Dr. Allen wants to cure Jane's anger he should give up Ms. Starks. She is also unwilling to force the children to go to family therapy and refuses to consent to any therapy that includes Ms. Starks. She states that Jane does not want anything to do with Dr. Allen or Ms. Starks and cannot be coerced into a relationship with either of them. Ms. Allen is willing to send the children to a neutral therapist provided that Dr. Allen pays for it. Although Dr. Allen is concerned about Jane's sudden weight loss, she isn't. She feels that Jane simply has lost her "baby fat," and she feels that Jane looks much better with her slimmer image. She is unconcerned about any of the health risks that Dr. Allen mentions, although she is open to hearing about this from the pediatrician, just not her husband.

When asked what the children need, she had a superficial focus on the issues. Most of her focus for the children had to do with her concerns about their reaction to the divorce. She feels that the children need her as their primary parent. She had little empathy for Dr. Allen's position that they need to have more time with him and a relationship with Ms. Starks. As mentioned above, she isn't worried about Jane's weight loss or her anger at her father, but she is worried about Joey's reaction to the divorce. She worries that Dr. Allen is trying to influence Joey to connect with Ms. Starks and ignore her. She also worries that Joey is overwhelmed with the divorce issues and won't adjust very well. Upon inquiry, Ms. Allen stated her willingness to have the children with their father every other weekend and one dinner visit weekly, as well as sharing of holidays and school breaks. She also indicated that each parent should have reasonable vacations with the children as requested when they are off from school. However, she again reiterated her belief that the children should not be "forced" to see their father, although she did acknowledge her responsibility to "encourage" the children to spend time with their dad.

THE CHILDREN

Jane Allen

Per both parent's reports, it appears that Jane was the product of a normal pregnancy and delivery. Developmental milestones were achieved within normal limits. Both parents report that she is interested in usual teen extracurricular activities, such as gymnastics, shopping, and boys. She is noted to be artistic and has a good sense of humor. Jane has always been a bright, but headstrong girl. In past years, when her parents' relationship seemed stable, she was intensely interested in school and friends. She was close to both parents, but not demonstratively affectionate. Recently, she has become critical of teachers and peers. She is heavily involved in gymnastics, and her teachers and her father became alarmed when she placed herself on a strict diet and began losing weight. She has stopped inviting friends home. Jane is very attached to her mother, and she vocally blames her father for her parents' marital difficulties and for "ruining" her life. She refuses to spend any time with her father. She has repeatedly told her parents and her friends that she intends to live with Ms. Allen no matter what the court decides.

Jane appears to this evaluator to be a bright, mildly depressed, but thoughtful girl who related reasonably well. She was hesitant to talk about her feelings, except for her anger at her father. She appears to be blaming him for the divorce, largely because of his affair with Ms. Starks. Jane tends toward being dramatic and talking in extremes, which is not unusual for an adolescent experiencing frustration at the breakup of her family. She is angry about the divorce because it is "ruining" her life and she wouldn't mind if she "never" saw her father again. She is also angry with her mother but wants to live with her because her mother has fewer rules than her father and lets her stay out with friends. Jane denies drug usage but acknowledges that her grades have suffered in the past few months. She described that she has been limiting her food intake because she feels "fat." She reports that she has lost about fifteen pounds over the past six months. She is unconcerned about this weight loss. She reports that she doesn't sleep very well, and that she doesn't get along well with Joey at the present time, in part because he loves his father and wants to live with him.

Jane talked a bit about the history of her family relationships. She used to enjoy spending time with her dad and was able to remember some enjoyable times with him when she was younger, but she clearly doesn't want to see him much now. She is glad that her mother doesn't "make" her see her father, adding, "to be honest, I don't really like her very much either. She's always at work and doesn't seem that interested in what I'm doing any more." As she talked more about all of this, she sounded quite sad. She denied being depressed and said that talking to her friends helps her with her feelings. She reports that she has never entertained suicidal thoughts, though she acknowledged feeling sad when she thinks about her life and how it's "falling apart." Like many sad-feeling teenagers going through a parenting evaluation, she was clear that she didn't want to talk about these issues and wanted to be left alone.

When seen with her mother, she was observed to be respectful and appropriate. She talked in a mature and relaxed manner and seemed to have a warm and relaxed relationship with her. She was polite to Joey during that observation. She made it clear that she wants to live with her mother. It is noted that Ms. Allen did nothing to encourage Jane to heal and resolve the issues between Jane and her father, or to spend time with her father despite her strong feelings.

In contrast, when seen with her father, she was observed to be rude and detached. She did not want to participate in discussions, and she was clearly angry with him. She blamed him for the divorce and sat in a sullen and nonresponsive manner, regardless of her father's efforts to engage her. She was also rude to Joey in that interview. It is noted that Dr. Allen was ineffective in efforts to engage with Jane or encourage her to treat Joey more reasonably.

Joey Allen

Per both parents' reports, it appears that Joey was also the product of a normal pregnancy and delivery. Developmental milestones were achieved within normal limits. Both parents report that he is interested in usual preteen activities, such as Little League, soccer, and video games. He has more friends than Jane. He is also noted to be playful and silly, and he has always had a good sense of humor.

Joey appears to this evaluator to be a rather shy, but self-confident boy who has always done extremely well in school and has had many friends. He usually admires his older sister, and in the past he has identified with her attitudes. But with the onset of the marital problems in the Allen household, Joey has come into increasing conflict with Jane. When Jane blames their father for the problems, Joey quarrels with her, especially when they are with their father. He reports that he sometimes tells Jane that their mother is to blame, but at other times he feels that both parents are to blame for the forthcoming divorce. He tries to restore balance in Jane's view of the parental conflicts. Joey complains frequently about Ms. Allen's being away at work in the evenings. Joey has also been having great difficulty sleeping—often waking with nightmares—and has recently wet the bed several times.

Joey appears to be a bit clingy. He was more open than Jane about his feelings and was more aware of the sadness that he feels. He loves both of his parents and doesn't want them to get divorced. He doesn't understand why they argue so much, and he doesn't like it when they do. He gets extremely frustrated with Jane and her angry attitude toward their father. Like many children involved in a parenting dispute between his parents, he was able to describe a number of things that he likes and dislikes about each of his parents. He hates it when his parents say bad things about each other, and he doesn't like it when his mother tries to get him to choose to live with her. Joey appears ambivalent about the parenting plan. For example, on one occasion, he insisted that if Dr. Allen moves away again, he wants to move with him. On another occasion, he said that he didn't care who he lives with, as long as he spends enough time with each of them. Such ambivalence is not unusual in children of divorce. Part of his ambivalence comes from feeling caught between his parents, which is more caused by his mother who appears to directly pressure him to want to stay with her.

There were few observed differences in the observations with his mother and his father. He was polite and affectionate with both and willing to talk about family issues. He was upset by Jane's treatment of their father, at times trying to get her to be nicer to him. There was no evidence of any particular problems in observing Joey's behavior or relationships with either parent.

Joey indicated that he likes school, but sometimes has a hard time concentrating. He used to do much better in school. He attributes the change to the divorce and his frustrations regarding his parents. His mother worries that Joey might be showing symptoms of ADHD, but Dr. Allen rejects that idea, believing that Joey simply is reacting to the divorce. We also talked about his interests in extracurricular activities. Like many youngsters his age, he is interested in sports and video games. This hasn't changed since the tension of the family, though he spends considerably more time playing video games than he used to. He has several close friends, one of whom also has divorced parents. However, he spends less time with his friends than he used to. Joey acknowledges that he's been more withdrawn and upset than he used to be, and he'd like it if his parents just settled the divorce

INTERVIEW WITH MS. NORMA STARKS AND HER CHILDREN

Ms. Starks was seen with her children, Kelly, age nine, and Jim, age eleven. As she talked, her affect was pleasant, and she stayed focused on the issues involved in the evaluation. They were all generally affectionate and at ease with one another as they talked about their relationships. There were no problems noted during the interview, including when talking about her former husband, who died four years ago of a brain tumor. She indicated, and the children confirmed, that she and the children had mourned the loss of her husband and that her major focus has always been on their well-being. For the first eighteen months after he died, she stayed home with the children. As things settled down for all of them, she went to work in her job with Dr. Allen.

Ms. Starks and the children talked about their relationships. All of them talked about how well they get along with each other. They miss their dad, and they talked about him and his death and how it had affected them. They have met Dr. Allen and like him, though they were clear that they don't feel he will ever replace their dad. Ms. Starks also indicated that he would not replace their dad but be a good stepfather to them. The children said that they like Joey, who enjoys playing with them, but they find Jane to be distant and sometimes "mean." They wish Jane would be nicer to them.

Both of the children were able to talk about things they liked about their mother. They find her to be funny, helpful, and "always there when we need her." They generally like her cooking, and Jim described that she helps him with his homework when he needs help. They discussed the family routine, one in which Ms. Starks wakes the children up at 6:30 in the morning for school, gets them breakfast, and helps get them ready. She takes them to school at 7:45 and goes to work. Both of the children go to after-school care until she picks them up at 5:00. The evening routine includes preparation for dinner, with the children helping; homework; and games or watching TV. The bedtime routine includes bathing, settling down and reading, and quiet talking. As they all talked about these routines, Ms. Starks and the children were silly and animated while talking about the games and reading that they do.

This evaluator talked with Ms. Starks about Joey and Jane. She enjoys her time with them and she believes that Dr. Allen is a "great father," explaining that he is sensitive to their feelings, dotes on them when they are all together, and gentle and kind with them. She reports that Dr. Allen is patient with Jane, even when Jane is angry at him for no apparent reason. Ms. Starks blames Ms. Allen for Jane's anger at Dr. Allen. She acknowledges that Joey has called her "Mom," saying that Joey made that decision, and, although she was uncomfortable at first, she decided not to make it an issue with Joey.

In all, Ms. Starks and her children appear to have wonderful relationships. They appear to have weathered the death of Mr. Starks reasonably well and, while the children still miss him, it appears that Ms. Starks has done an excellent job of meeting their needs. There was no evidence of any problems in their relationships noted in this interview.

COLLATERAL CONTACTS

Dr. Sturm (Ms. Allen's therapist)

Dr. Sturm did not want to divulge too much information about the clinical work between him and Ms. Allen. He did report that she has been coming for sessions on average every other week for about a year. They discuss the divorce issues and other "personal" issues that are relevant in her life. He believes that Ms. Allen is committed to her children and wants what is best for them. When they discuss parenting issues, he believes that she understands the children's needs, in particular their needs for stability and consistency in their lives. He talks with her about reducing the conflicts with Dr. Allen, and he is trying to help her understand and deal with her feelings related to Ms. Starks. He could think of no reason why she should not receive strong consideration as the primary parent for these children.

Dr. Paulson (School Psychologist)

Dr. Paulson expressed considerable concern about both of the children. Jane has been losing weight and appears overwhelmed and depressed. Joey has become more withdrawn. Both children appear to be doing worse academically. He has sent a letter of her concerns, which is in the collateral information all sides have. Both parents met with Dr. Paulson and the rest of the school team to discuss the children and their respective issues. The school made a number of suggestions. They included therapy and tutoring for the children. The parents arranged tutoring, but they decided to wait until this evaluation is completed before deciding how to proceed about therapy. Until their recent stressors, Dr. Paulson felt that both parents had been doing a good job with the children. He does not have an opinion about the specific parenting plan, but instead hopes that the children's needs can once again become the paramount concern of both parents.

Dr. Henne (Pediatrician)

Dr. Henne has been the children's pediatrician since Jane's birth. She reports that the children have always been in good health and have had no particular problems. While both parents have taken responsibility for routine medical appointments, Dr. Henne has always felt a greater connection with Dr. Allen. When asked about Jane's recent weight loss, Dr. Henne expressed that she is becoming concerned because Jane has lost nearly fifteen pounds in the past six months. Jane is 5 feet 1 inch tall and weighs 102 pounds. While this weight is in the 5th percentile for her height, Jane is very interested in gymnastics, and Dr. Henne noted that many of her female gymnastics patients tend to be thin. Dr. Henne did feel that Jane's weight should be carefully monitored, and she would be increasingly concerned if Jane's weight drops below 100 pounds.

Supportive Letters of Family and Friends on Behalf of Both Parents

Without summarizing each letter, it is sufficient to report that all three letters sent on behalf of Dr. Allen and all three letters sent on behalf of Ms. Allen were quite positive and suggested that each parent has many adequate parenting skills and few deficits.

ADDITIONAL ISSUES FOR THE COURT

Domestic Violence

There was no history of domestic violence in this family. Dr. and Ms. Allen have managed to resolve conflicts without resorting to violence. After thorough discussion with each parent and review of the file, there is no evidence of any pattern or history of control or dominance by either parent toward the other.

Health and Special Need Issues of the Children

As indicated above, there is some concern about Jane's recent weight loss, though Dr. Henne is not overly concerned if her weight stabilizes now. It is respectfully recommended that Jane's weight continue to be monitored. If her weight loss continues or her weight does not stabilize after the settlement of this case, the parents should discuss options for addressing her weight loss with the person assigned to improve their communication and problem solving (see Recommendation 3, later in this report).

While there has been some question about Joey's school difficulties, there has been no evidence of any historical school problems. Thus, I see no reason for a referral for ADHD or any other such issues at this time.

Mediation

Mediation has so far been unsuccessful. Both parents have mistrusted one another and do not communicate well. They have not been able to solve their difficulties, despite the fact that each of them recognize the difficulties each of their children are experiencing. Despite this, they will need some type of co-parenting assistance moving forward. Despite the failures of mediation early in this divorce process, this evaluator believes that the parties will benefit from someone to facilitate their communication and problem solving on behalf of the children.

ANALYSIS, SUMMARY, AND RECOMMENDATIONS

As is common in child custody evaluations, both Dr. and Ms. Allen have a variety of strengths and weaknesses related to their parenting and co-parenting, and both have emotional issues that are contributing to the problems being experienced. In addition, each of them has more awareness of their partner's respective contribution to the problems than their own, as each of them has limited insight into his or her contributions to the problems. I will start with their strengths.

Ms. Allen has, until recently, been a primary, stay-at-home mother, and during the time that she was in this role, she did a very effective job. The children functioned well, and during that time period of the Allen marriage, there were no particular problems. At the same time, history reveals that Dr. Allen also contributed to raising the children, as he participated daily in their relationships and with important school and extracurricular activities. Both of them have been very loving, attentive, and affectionate, and while there are some basic differences in the way they relate and communicate, each of them has been warm and supportive of their children's emotions, academics, friendships, and psychological well-being.

However, in recent years, as Ms. Allen became more involved in her work, Dr. Allen became more of the main caregiver. While he has been involved with Ms. Starks, he came home when asked to by Ms. Allen to watch the children and became more involved in their daily routine.

Over the last few years, Ms. Allen became more focused on her career than the children. Even though she continues to be the primary day-to-day parent, she has lost sight of Jane's need for guidance and direction as it relates to her eating and doesn't seem to recognize how her own anger and frustration with Dr. Allen has contributed to Jane's anger, withdrawal, and negative feelings toward her father. If she were more secure in her own parenting role at this time, her feelings about Ms. Starks wouldn't be such a big issue for her. Both parents are aware that Joey is having difficulties, but neither of them is working to help him resolve those problems. Ultimately, neither parent is focused enough on how the children are doing today, as evidenced by the problems noted above.

At the moment, it appears that each parent has some personality attributes that are negatively impacting parenting and their ability to resolve their dispute. Dr. Allen at times is very self-centered, but this is not unusual when one is going through a divorce and involved with another person. This makes it more difficult to resolve his dispute with his wife and makes it harder for him to see that he has not always put the children's needs first. Ms. Allen's anger, outrage, and overreaction are the main characteristics that impede her ability to resolve the dispute between the parties. It is also negatively impacting the children, as she has been exhibiting some behaviors consistent with restrictive gatekeeping and is attempting to undermine the children's relationship with their father. Each of them acts as if the other is unimportant when seeking to be the primary parent, and at the present time, both Dr. and Ms. Allen are relatively oblivious to the causes of the children's suffering. History reveals that the children have done best when both parents have contributed to their well-being. However, at this point in time it will be difficult for the Allens to successfully share parenting time, given their animosity and poor communication. It will be difficult to arrange this after the divorce without a great deal of assistance for them. Although it would be best for the children to have both parents involved in their day-to-day lives and functioning, a parenting plan in which the children spend equal time with each parent is not likely to be successful, given the dynamics of the parents.

Consideration of Factors Affecting the Welfare and Interests of the Child

(a) The parent who is more likely to allow the child frequent and continuing contact with the nonresidential parent.

It is this examiner's opinion that this factor weighs to the benefit of Dr. Allen. Both parents state that they support the children's relationship with the other parent. However, Ms. Allen states she will do so only as long as the children want such contact. While they each blame the other, it is likely that once this dispute is settled, both will support the children's relationship with the other parent to a greater degree than now. However, I am concerned that Ms. Allen may support Jane's resistance toward her father and may be willing to allow her to refuse contact with her father if things continue to worsen between Jane and her father. Ideally, both parents will recognize the need for the children to have and maintain frequent and continuing contact with the other parent.

(b) The love, affection, and other emotional ties existing between the parents and the child.

As noted above, both parents enjoy love, affection, and strong emotional ties with the children. It is this examiner's opinion that the reciprocal bond between the children and each parent is relatively equal. While Jane currently prefers her mother and Joey currently prefers his father, the attachments are strong for all of them.

(c) The capacity of the parent to provide the child with food, clothing, medical care or other remedial care recognized and permitted under the laws of this state in lieu of medical care, and other material need.

Both parents have demonstrated the ability to provide the children with food, clothing, medical care, and other basic needs through the remainder of their childhood, and I am confident that this will continue.

(d) The length of time the child has lived in a stable, satisfactory environment and the desirability of maintaining continuity.

The Allen children have lived consistently under the care and guidance of both parents. Although Ms. Allen was the more hands-on parent earlier in their lives, Dr. Allen has become more actively involved in their day-to-day lives in recent years. To maintain continuity of this arrangement, it will be best if both parents remain active in their day-to-day lives.

(e) The permanence, as a family unit, of the existing or proposed custodial home.

The children have lived in their current home for the bulk of their childhood. They have a good relationship with one other, and there is no reason for them to be separated.

(f) *The moral fitness of the parents.*

The ability to detect the moral fitness of a parent is beyond the scope of practice of a forensic psychologist. Morality is a subjective determination and relies on the suspension of objectivity, and at times fact. The question may be better addressed in terms of the parents' behavior and psychological composition as it influences the children, to wit . . .

(g) *The mental and physical health of the parents.*

As noted above, each parent has more strengths than weaknesses in their respective psychological health, and both tend toward authoritative, healthier parenting when they are focused on the children and their needs. While both parents have personality traits that impact and affect parenting and their co-parenting relationship in different ways, there is no evidence to suggest that either parent has any mental or physical health issues that would render one or the other more (or less) capable of meeting the children's needs, with the possible exception of Ms. Allen's level of anger, which causes her to exhibit restrictive gatekeeping behaviors and is undermining the children's relationship with their father, and concerns about her use of alcohol.

(h) *The home, school, and community record of the child.*

By and large, except for the temporary difficulties Joey has been experiencing, both children have functioned well in their home, school, and community. There have been some adjustment issues associated with the recent changes and conflicts within the family, but they generally show evidence of strong and healthy functioning.

(i) *The history of interparental conflict, including any incidents of domestic violence.*

As noted in the report, Dr. and Ms. Allen had a fairly low-conflict marriage, until conflict escalated in the last year or two prior to their temporary separation. Since their temporary separation, they have been in more heated verbal conflict and have struggled to communicate effectively and make joint decisions on behalf of the children. There has been no coercive control by either parent, nor have there been any acts of physical, emotional, sexual, or economic violence. In the midst of their conflict, there has been limited, though mutual, verbal abuse and name-calling. Neither parent is fearful of the other, and there is no history of domestic violence.

Risk/Benefit Analysis of Various Parenting Plan Options

Given the absence of domestic violence, child maltreatment, and substance abuse issues in this case, the remaining questions center on the risks and benefits of the mother as the primary parent, the father as primary parent, and both parents equally sharing parenting time. It is this examiner's opinion that as we consider these options, the risks and benefits of each option are very close. The chief benefit of the father as primary parent would be that it would force Jane to deal with her feelings toward him and force a situation in which they find a way to resolve their differences. He also appears to have a better understanding of her current eating issues. Furthermore, he is more supportive of the children being involved with their mother than the reverse. He is also not attempting to undermine the children's relationship with the other parent. However, the risks of the father as primary parent are that Ms. Starks might act as if she is the de facto primary parent and be insensitive to how that will affect the children's relationship with their mother. Another concern is that Jane does not enjoy time with her father and does not even want to go with him half of the time. Jane also does not like Ms. Starks and her children. Finally, Dr. Allen is so focused on his preference to build a new life with Ms. Starks that he tends to minimize the importance of Ms. Allen in the children's lives.

The primary benefits of the mother as primary parent are continuing the potential for her day-to-day primary role. Along with this, Jane would be happier because she would be able to avoid dealing with the issues with her father. However, the risks are found in the fact that Ms. Allen is spending increasing time at work away from home and therefore is less focused on and less prepared to meet the children's current day-to-day needs. In addition, she has little awareness or insight into Jane's eating difficulties, and she is, at best, struggling to support Jane's relationship with her father.

This leads to the option of shared residence. The primary benefit of such an arrangement is that the children will have access to both parents on a regular and consistent basis and continue the pattern in which both parents participate actively in the caregiving. Just as if Dr. Allen had primary residence, the prospect of shared residence will force Jane and her father to resolve their issues, and it would give them a day-to-day opportunity to renew and improve their relationship. Along with this, research generally suggests that most children benefit when two parents stay actively involved in a wide range of their children's life experiences and activities in an atmosphere of low conflict and high communication. In those circumstances, a shared parenting arrangement is often ideal.

However, in this examiner's opinion, the risks in such a plan outweigh any benefit that might come from shared residence. While it appears that Dr. and Ms. Allen would do well to share parental responsibilities, equally shared parenting time usually does not work for two parents with such poor communication and high levels of conflict. If both could renew their past parenting practices and rebuild their style such that they love the children more than they dislike each other and keep the primary focus and sacrifice on raising their children, this risk could be minimized. However, I am concerned that they will continue to argue about therapists, educational issues, Jane and her functioning, etc. For this reason, I believe that shared residence will not work at the present time. Only if the litigation settles down would such an arrangement work.

Thus, given that Dr. Allen has been more involved in recent years with the children and is more supportive of the children's relationship with their mother than the reverse, he should be the primary parent and the children should see Ms. Allen on a regular and consistent schedule. While most of the factors are relatively equal, it is this examiner's opinion that Ms. Allen's level of anger, restrictive gatekeeping, and attempts to undermine the children's relationship with their father outweigh the fact that she has been the main caregiver of the children throughout the majority of their lives. Given these issues, it is in the children's best interests if Dr. Allen is the primary parent. Furthermore, it will allow Jane and her father to work on their relationship. Also, as Dr. Allen stated, he will stay in the same school district; living primarily with him will not alter the children's adjustment to their school and community.

RECOMMENDATIONS

Given all of the above, I offer the following recommendations:

1. Dr. Allen and Ms. Allen should continue sharing parental responsibility. Based upon Dr. Allen's greater appreciation of Jane's eating problems, his greater day-to-day availability, and the challenges with the mother's limited support of the children's relationship with their father, the children should spend the majority of their time with Dr. Allen. This would enable the children to continue in their current community with no disruption in their day-to-day lives. I recommend that the children see their mother every other

Thursday from after school until Monday morning. In weeks when the children do not see their mother over the weekend from Thursday after school through Monday morning, they would be with their mother overnight on Thursday nights.

2. Both parents should refrain from making any derogatory statements about one other to, or in front of, the children. Such statements reinforce Jane's oppositional behavior and continue the extent to which she remains affected by their conflicts. While Joey appears less affected outwardly, I suspect this is contributing to his withdrawal.

3. Even after these issues are settled, a professional should be appointed to assist these parents in resolving their ongoing disputes. Given their current distrust and difficulties, I recommend that they use either a parenting coordinator (if they can stipulate to one) or a co-parent counselor to discuss any disputes involving the children's care and well-being. I would discourage both parents from engaging in conflict within the children's earshot; use the mediator or parenting coordinator to settle such disputes. All efforts should be made by both parents to use this professional to keep the children out of the middle of their disputes.

4. Given the issues noted above, the children should participate in a therapeutic group program, something that is useful as an adjunct to resolving conflicts associated with parents' divorce. Along with this, however, both parents should continue to watch for signs in which the children need individual therapy. If Jane's eating issues don't resolve themselves soon, I'd certainly recommend evaluation and treatment for that.

5. Emergency or timely information must be communicated by phone, but otherwise, there should be limited contact between the parents. I would hope that the professional assisting them will help them develop their parallel parenting style. In fact, the appropriate use of a parenting coordinator or co-parent counselor and the disengagement of the parents are the most important things that these parents can do to help the children. Each of them needs to focus more on his or her own parenting and learn to be less critical of the other. If they can learn to resolve their disputes away from the children and work toward being the best parent each can be during the times he or she has the children, almost any time-share in which both parents are actively involved will be workable and successful.

6. I recommend that the parents communicate via Nita Family Resource (www.nitafamilyresource.nita). This secure mobile application will allow the parents to communicate with one another, schedule parenting time, and share information without involving the children.

7. In the event the parents continue to remain in conflict and things do not stabilize, a brief updated evaluation would be indicated.

Thank you for allowing me to be of assistance with this family.

Pat Nolan

Pat Nolan, PhD
Nita Licensed Psychologist

Date of Report: May 1, YR-0

PAT NOLAN, PhD

OFFICE ADDRESS	777 Washington Blvd., Suite 225 Nita City, Nita 09999 V/M: (555) 555-5555 & Fax: (555) 555-6666 Email: pnolan@nitagreatshrink.nita
EDUCATION	AGP University, PhD in Clinical Psychology, August, YR-10. AGP University, BS in History, May, YR-14.
FELLOWSHIP &	Clinical Psychology Intern, Nita Mental Health Institute,
INTERNSHIP	YR-10 to YR-9 (APA approved Internship)
LICENSE	Licensed Psychologist, State of Nita
PUBLICATIONS	Nolan, P. (YR-7) "The Importance of Parent Education for Divorcing Parents," *Nita Family Courts Review*, Vol. 35(2), pp. 223–238. Nolan, P. (YR-4) "Parental Conflict and Children of Divorce," *Nita Family Courts Review*, Vol. 38(1), pp. 28–43. Nolan, P. (YR-2) "The Concept of Father's Rights in the Context of Maternal Gatekeeping in High-Conflict Family Law Cases," *Nita Family Courts Review*, Vol. 40(2), pp. 221–242.
MEMBERSHIPS	Member, Nita Association of Family Courts Member, Nita Psychological Association
EXPERIENCE	
9/YR-7 to present:	Clinical Psychology Practice including individual and family psychotherapy, forensic psychology, and mental health
9/YR-10 to 9/YR-7:	Assistant Professor, AGP University, Nita, USA
AWARDS	Phi Beta Kappa, YR-14 Outstanding Teacher Award, AGP University, YR-2
TRAINING	Dr. Nolan has attended over seventy hours of advanced continuing education in the areas of parenting evaluation, forensic evaluation of children, divorce, and family mediation. In addition, Pat Nolan, PhD, has presented at numerous conferences including the Nita Association Family Courts and the Nita Psychological Association.

PRIOR TESTIMONY Since YR-4, Dr. Nolan has been appointed as an evaluator by the court in approximately seventy-five family law matters across four jurisdictions. Dr. Nolan has testified in six depositions and four trials.

FEE SCHEDULES Dr. Nolan's fees are as follows:

- Custody Evaluations — $300/hour
- Deposition Testimony — $350/hour (including time for preparation) + travel time
- Trial Testimony — $400/hour (including time for preparation) + travel time

CONFIDENTIAL MATERIALS FOR PETITIONER'S COUNSEL

Memorandum

To: *Allen v. Allen* file
From: Counsel
Re: Summary of background facts

This memorandum summarizes the background facts of *Allen* v. *Allen* as learned from our client, David Allen, and review of documents that he provided. It includes impressions of counsel.

The Allen's Marriage and Children

In the summer of YR-16, about seven months after his relationship with a nurse ended, David Allen met Lynne Grant, who was a patient representative. They began meeting for coffee to discuss the progress of his patients. The conversations soon turned to more general discussions of medicine and of David's interest in developing a radiology practice after finishing his residency. David reports that he was very charmed by Lynne and flattered by her attention to his future goals. They would spend long hours going over his research results. Lynne helped edit his research reports and also helped write and edit his first published article.

In the fall of YR-16, David asked Lynne to marry him. He felt that since his career seemed to be going very well, he was ready to settle down. Lynne and David married on February 2, YR-15. When they married, both David and Lynne assumed they would have children. David felt that they should begin their family only when they were on secure financial footing.

In the summer of YR-14, David finished his residency and fellowship. He decided to open a private radiology practice. Lynne helped him plan the practice in detail and provided emotional support for his future plans. She helped design the office space and hire staff. She also entertained at dinners for potential referral sources such as hospital administrators and other doctors. The practice flourished.

David and Lynne decided they were financially secure enough to begin their family. Their first child, Jane, was born in YR-13. In YR-11, a second child, Joey, was born. Lynne agreed to stay home with the children until they reached school age. David says Lynne did this somewhat reluctantly, as she feared the social isolation and lack of adult and community contact that might result from staying at home full time. However, she found great satisfaction in motherhood and became active in the community.

By YR-10, with Jane approaching preschool and Joey about to start toddling, Lynne and David decided to leave their Nita City apartment and move to the suburbs. They purchased a large older home in Huntington, Nita (an attractive suburb), close to where David's parents lived, which Lynne began fixing up.

Lynne Allen's Return to School and Entrance into the Workforce

By YR-6, with Joey in kindergarten, Lynne felt she wanted to complete her degree and return to the working world. Lynne transferred her Bennington credits to Nita University, where she could commute to classes and complete her BA on a part-time basis. She changed her major to communications, and through her course work she became involved in programming at WNUR, the campus radio station.

In YR-4, Lynne received her BA in communications. Through her community activities, she became friends with a woman who sold advertising time on a twenty-four-hour news format radio station.

Lynne's friend put her in touch with several people in management at local radio stations. Lynne's networking eventually produced an offer from a small commercial station that she admired, WKJW, whose studios are near Nita University. The station featured a mixed bag of information and music, appealing to upwardly mobile, middle-class tastes. Lynne accepted a part-time position with the station in the programming and feature development department.

David states he was pleased that Lynne had completed her college degree. He did, however, express some ambivalence about her return to work. While he understood her desire to reestablish an identity separate from wife and mother and to prepare for the inevitable day when Jane and Joey grew up, he worried what effect it would have on the children.

Once Lynne started working, David believed she became much less supportive of him and his work. In the evening, after the children were in bed, he thought she was often more interested in catching up on her paperwork and discussing programming ideas with him than in sharing the ups and downs of his practice. David said Lynne was focusing more energy and attention on work and less on Jane and Joey. Lynne recognized David's concerns and feelings about her career but felt he would eventually adjust.

David states he had always been an active parent to his children, taking them on outings and supervising their homework. As a doctor, David took responsibility for the children's medical care. Before going to work at the radio station, Lynne was responsible for such things as cooking meals, feeding and bathing the children, putting them to bed, and getting up with them in the night. When Lynne started working, David states he adjusted his schedule and became more involved with the day-to-day care of the children, spending more of his evenings with Jane and Joey and fewer evenings with his journals and practice development details.

Meanwhile, David states that Lynne claims to have continued to devote a substantial amount of time and energy to caring for the children. She was insistent that they not be "shortchanged" by her return to work. She found her new schedule left her frazzled, with less time than she liked for interests other than her work and her children. Lynne, however, felt invigorated by her job. She found she had a keen sense for radio work and earned increasing responsibility at the station. She told David that she felt she had given her "all" to her family for thirteen years and was now ready to grow in other ways.

In the fall of YR-3, Lynne accepted a full-time position as assistant programming director of WKJW. Her programming duties expanded, and she now had control of "new feature" development. The salary—$30,000—was small for the position, but Lynne felt that she would miss a rare opportunity to gain experience should she pass it up.

The Deterioration of the Allen's Marriage

David started to feel Lynne was barely managing to have time for her work and the children. Their relationship was left completely out of the equation. David states that by this point Lynne and David's communications were limited. Their previously active sex life deteriorated dramatically. David made statements that Lynne interpreted as showing signs that he resented her career, while Lynne felt his resentment was unreasonable. David says Lynne became withdrawn and avoided discussing their marital problems. This caused David to yell at her. Lynne told David he didn't take her feelings or her career seriously. David seems to have responded by becoming even angrier, saying he didn't know what Lynne's feelings were since she never discussed them.

Three years ago, further strain was placed on the Allen's' marriage when Lynne was promoted to full-time assistant programming director. David's comments, far from easing the tension, made Lynne increasingly angry. She chose to direct even more of her time and energy into her work. On a number of occasions in late YR-3, Lynne called David at work, saying that he needed to take care of Jane and Joey so that she could work late at the station. More than once, this required David to leave his practice responsibilities to take care of the children. Twice, Lynne arrived home very late with alcohol on her breath. She made light of the matter when David commented, saying that she had merely had a drink with dinner to relax. While she had not seemed intoxicated, David was alarmed since previously Lynne rarely drank. David suspects that Lynne's evening activity can only be explained by her being involved with someone else.

David confided his problems with Lynne to Norma Starks, his x-ray technician. Norma is a widow raising two children. David and Norma spent many hours working together. Through their conversations, David learned how involved Norma was with her children. David was impressed by her ability to excel at her profession and at parenthood. David was flattered by Norma's attention, particularly because he felt Lynne had emotionally abandoned him. Norma supported his career in the same way that Lynne had once provided. David confided in Norma that he and Lynne were having problems. He told her that Lynne was preoccupied with her own life and that she refused to reduce her career involvement to spend more time with David. Shortly after David confided that he was having marital problems, he and Norma began an affair and sexual relationship. This was in YR-3, while Lynne was spending an increasing amount of her time at work.

Norma had worked for David since YR-4, making a salary of $70,000. She is currently thirty-seven years old. Widowed after her husband succumbed to a protracted battle with cancer, Norma was raising her two children, ages nine and eleven by herself. She was the president of her children's school's PTA and a Girl Scouts troop leader. She was involved in all the activities of her children, a quality that impressed David. He knew that it was not easy for a single parent to raise two children successfully without any assistance. Although the Starks children miss their father, they do well in home and at school.

During one particularly heated argument with Lynne in January YR-2, David told Lynne about his affair with Norma and announced he wanted a divorce, so he could continue his involvement openly. After David admitted his affair to Lynne, he left the marital residence and stayed with Norma in her apartment in Nita City.

This living arrangement continued for about a month. David moved back into the marital residence, where he currently lives with Lynne and the children. David told Lynne he moved back in because he didn't want their marital difficulties to harm his relationship with the children, a harm he feared would be compounded if he lived out of the house.

David sleeps in the guest bedroom in the house, and Lynne sleeps in the bedroom they once shared. David spends several nights each week at Norma's apartment. The children know their parents are having marital problems and have overheard them arguing. There is no history of domestic violence between David and Lynne.

The Effect of Marital Problems on the Allen Children

David thinks that Lynne is very angry about Norma's "breaking up" the family and will never accept her as playing any role in the children's lives. Her attitude towards Norma and David is described in a recent Facebook post by Lynne (Exhibit 8).

David rejected Lynne's suggestions they go to counseling, saying that their relationship is over. Lynne told David she is in therapy, meeting weekly with a psychologist whose office is near her radio station. She told David the focus of her therapy is an attempt to work out the tension she feels between balancing career concerns and family responsibilities.

Lynne also periodically suggests that David move out again. David continues to refuse these requests. There is significant tension in the house. David spends some weeknight evenings at Norma's apartment (he tells Lynne in advance so that someone will be home with the children), but most nights he sleeps in the family residence.

Jane and Joey spend Wednesday evenings and every other weekend with David. David tries to spend this time with Jane, but she refuses to participate in any activities with him. The parties agreed to this temporary parenting schedule.

The children are not doing well. David says that daughter Jane has always been a bright, but headstrong girl. In past years when her parents' relationship seemed stable, she was intensely interested in school and friends. She was close to both parents.

Recently, she has become critical of her teachers and peers. She is actively involved in gymnastics, and her teachers and David became alarmed when she placed herself on a strict diet and began losing weight. Over the past three months, she has lost nearly fifteen pounds. Jane is now five feet one inch tall and has lost sufficient weight to be 102 pounds. There is some concern she is exhibiting signs of an eating disorder. She has stopped inviting friends home. Jane is very close to Lynne, and she vocally blames her father for her parents' marital difficulties and refuses to spend any time with him. She has repeatedly told the family that she intends to live with Lynne no matter what happens.

David is worried that Lynne is not concerned enough about Jane's weight loss and is discouraging Jane from spending time with him. He points to a recent text exchange between Lynne and Jane as supporting his view (Exhibit 4).

According to David, Joey is a rather shy but self-confident boy who does extremely well in school and has many friends. He usually admires his older sister. In the past, he has identified with her attitudes. With the onset of the marital problems in the Allen household, Joey has come into increasing conflict with Jane. When Jane blames their father for the problems, Joey quarrels with her, saying Lynne is to blame or that both are to blame. Joey complains frequently about Lynne being away at work in the evenings. Joey insists that if David moves away again, he wants to move away with him. Joey also is now having great difficulty sleeping—often waking with nightmares—and he has wet the bed several times.

The children have met Norma and her children on several occasions. Jane had a significant negative reaction to Norma and does not want to spend time with her. Lynne raised Jane's reluctance to be with David with her. Jane reluctantly told Lynne about a conversation with Norma that greatly upset Jane. According to Jane, Norma recently told Jane and Joey they should "think of me as a second mother" and "feel free to call me 'Mom.' " Jane told Lynne that Norma offered to take her to the mall to buy clothes. Jane asked Lynne, "Mom, am I losing you?"

Lynne then asked Joey about this conversation. Joey confirmed that it occurred. He also said, however, that Norma was friendly, sweet, and "cool," and she seemed very interested in both him and Jane. He reported getting along well with Norma and her children.

Lynne raised this incident with David. He told her that Jane's reaction was simply the result of her over-identification with Lynne. David explained to Lynne that after the divorce and his marriage to Norma, the children would indeed have two mothers. Lynne became furious at this statement and stomped out of the room. Since this initial discussion, the subject has not been raised again.

David and Lynne recently received a letter from Joey and Jane's school psychologist (Exhibit 1). The psychologist indicated the children's teachers expressed concern about the children's behavior, in particular Jane's belligerence towards her teachers, her weight loss, and her recent falling grades. These concerns were also stated in a letter from the academic dean at Jane's school, who expressed them in a letter to David and Lynne shortly after the psychologist's letter (Exhibit 2). Jane's recent report card, too, is worrisome (Exhibit 3). When David and Lynne then met with relevant school personnel, this information was confirmed.

As a result, David and Lynne agreed that Jane should have tutoring. They could not agree, though, on therapy for the children. David wanted to refer the children to someone he believed to be a well-qualified therapist but who is a colleague of David's at Nita Medical Center. The colleague will accept less than the going rate for therapy. David claims his medical insurance does not provide for substantial mental health coverage for the kids. Lynne, however, will not agree to the children having therapy with David's colleague because she feels he will encourage the children to side with David over her.

David also believes that Lynne is preventing Jane and Joey from developing a relationship with Norma and her children. He was particularly angry when Lynne refused to allow Jane and Joey to take a weekend trip to watch Norma's son play in a baseball championship game upstate with a sightseeing tour to follow (Exhibit 6).

Lynne Allen's Career

In February YR-2, Lynne presented the WKJW managing board with a new feature proposal for their 1:00 PM weekday slot. Lynne told David that the "time slot had been a thorn in the side of station management for some time, plagued by low ratings and declining advertising revenues." Lynne proposed trying a sports program with a new angle. The show's pitch would be to "baseball widows"—women with husbands so obsessively involved with sports the wives feel "widowed" during the season. The program would cover college and pro ball, highlighting current action and providing background and education about the sport. Construction of features would be from a woman's perspective, in a slightly humorous vein.

The station accepted the proposal and suggested Lynne host the show. Lynne created the concept and possessed the requisite sports knowledge to be successful. While Lynne's father instilled in her his passion for baseball, taking her to many games in her youth, Lynne maintained her interest in sports throughout her adult life; though not as fervent as her father, she remained an active spectator. Lynne, David, and the children often attended the major-league Nita City Cubs games, and Lynne avidly reads books, articles, blogs, statistics, and other baseball information.

Baseball Widows has its own Facebook page (Exhibit 7). The show had its broadcast debut as spring training commenced in YR-1. By late summer, the audience was at an all-time high for the time slot, with positive effects for WKJW's other programs as new listeners tuned in. Fourth quarter YR-1 advertising revenues for this previously difficult time slot showed so dramatic an increase that the large local stations noticed. Early this year, Lynne and WKJW received several offers to market *Baseball Widows* nationally. She is currently entering negotiations with several radio networks. This may be the major turning point in her radio career. She could receive a raise in the near future and be making upwards of $50,000 a year.

David feels that Lynne is "wrapped up" in her career and has stopped caring for the children and him. He points to a number of occasions where Lynne called him on very short notice to take care of the children. (See the email exchange between them in Exhibit 5.) At times, Lynne has come home late smelling of alcohol, which David attributes to late "business dinners" with someone Lynne is having an affair with. The affair was confirmed in a Facebook post by Lynne (Exhibit 8).

Memorandum

To: *Allen v. Allen* file
From: Counsel
Re: Client instructions re: commencing divorce action
Date: March 1, YR-1

I met with Dr. Allen today. Dr. Allen authorized us to commence an action for divorce against Ms. Allen. He feels that they will never be able to reach agreement on parenting issues or on a financial settlement without going to court. He wants more time with the children than Ms. Allen will accept, and they cannot agree on the therapist for the children who he recommends. We agreed that he would tell Ms. Allen that he is commencing an action for divorce so that she will not feel blindsided and can retain counsel (if she has not already).

Dr. Allen reemphasized his desire for a quick resolution of the dispute, so his divorce can be final and he can marry Ms. Starks.

The complaint for divorce was filed on March 21, YR-1, and served upon Ms. Allen that same day.

Memorandum

To: *Allen v. Allen* file
From: Counsel
Re: Client objectives in parenting dispute
Date: November YR-0

This memorandum summarizes Dr. Allen's current thoughts on possible parenting plans for Joey, age ten, and Jane, age thirteen, in anticipation of settlement negotiation and mediation.

Shortly after Dr. Allen's complaint and Ms. Allen's counterclaim for divorce were filed and served, they agreed upon a parenting schedule. Jane and Joey are with David every other weekend and on Wednesday evenings. Dr. Allen does not feel that this schedule gives him adequate time with Jane and Joey. He agreed to it to avoid a premature court hearing that would put the children in the middle. He feels, however, that the situation has become intolerable, especially because he believes that Ms. Allen is encouraging Jane not to have anything to do with him. He also thinks that Ms. Allen's position on not sending the children to his colleague for therapy is unreasonable and that Ms. Allen is insufficiently concerned about Jane's weight loss.

Dr. Allen wants to be the primary decision maker for the children and have the children spend the majority of time with him. He recognizes that Ms. Allen is an important figure in the children's lives and is willing to afford her reasonable visitation and input into key decisions but believes he should retain decision-making authority. He does not think he has enough time with the children under the current residence arrangements.

Dr. Allen is also worried about Jane and Joey's changes in behavior. He is concerned that Jane is much too thin and may have an eating disorder. The fact that Lynne tells Jane that she looks better now troubles him. Joey's difficulty sleeping and withdrawn behavior in class are not like him.

Dr. Allen is happy with the tutor for Jane that he and Lynne agreed on after meeting with the school psychologist and the "team" at the children's school. He also wants the children to be in therapy but is concerned about its cost. Dr. Allen has a colleague who will provide therapy at reduced rates. Since his insurance does not cover psychological counseling, working with his colleague will make the therapy affordable for Dr. Allen. If they go to another provider, Dr. Allen wants Lynne to pay half of the costs.

Dr. Allen states that living with Ms. Allen under the same roof is stressful, and he wants to resolve the situation as soon as possible. He is willing to let Ms. Allen have the marital home once the divorce is finalized.

Dr. Allen thinks that Ms. Allen is unduly influencing Jane's opinion of Ms. Starks and of him. Jane currently refuses to spend any time with her father, a matter of great concern to him. Dr. Allen believes Ms. Allen fuels this animosity with negative remarks about Ms. Starks, blaming her for the dissolution of their marriage. Dr. Allen thus believes it is in the children's best interests to develop a relationship with Ms. Starks and that there should not be restrictions on that relationship. He thinks that Ms. Starks will be a great stepparent for the children.

DR. JUDY FRACK'S REPORT
EVALUATING DR. PAT NOLAN'S PARENTING EVALUATION
(FOR DR. DAVID ALLEN'S COUNSEL ONLY)

ATTORNEY WORK PRODUCT

Dr. Judy Frack[*]

June 1, YR-0

Jamie Lederman
Nita Bar Building, Suite 333
Nita City, Nita 09995

Memo: Summary of concerns regarding Dr. Nolan's report from Consultant

Ms. Lederman:

I am writing this memo as your confidential consultant, hired to share my observations of the strengths and weaknesses of Dr. Nolan's report in the Allen matter in anticipation of Dr. Nolan's testimony at deposition and trial. As we discussed, I will not be called as a witness at trial.

In order of importance, here are what I see as the strengths of Dr. Nolan's report (you should, of course, note that some of the strengths have corresponding weaknesses as well):

- Dr. Nolan utilized a multi-method process with interviews of the parties, interviews of the children, observations of the children and each of their parents, reviews of collateral information, interviews with collateral witnesses, all leading to a report focusing on the statutory factors.
- Dr. Nolan provided an analysis identifying risks and benefits of various custodial options and explained the rationale for giving father primary custody of the children.
- Dr. Nolan generally seemed balanced in approach/procedures.

In order of importance, here are what I see as the weaknesses of Dr. Nolan's report:

- There is a general lack of depth in much of Dr. Nolan's assessment, which increases the risks that Dr. Nolan's conclusions are speculative and of limited usefulness.
- Dr. Nolan did a poor assessment and analysis of each parent's respective gatekeeping behaviors. Gatekeeping refers to a parent's facilitation of the relationship with the other parent. It occurs along a continuum and has multiple dimensions, including support of the child's relationship with the other parent (or lack thereof); qualities of communication (or problems in such); extent to which the parent encourages input on major decision-making (or marginalizes the other parent); extent to which the parent speaks positively

[*] Dr. Frack is a licensed psychologist in the State of Nita who has been a forensic psychologist for over twenty-five years. She has conducted nearly 700 custody evaluations by court appointment; has written extensively on child custody matters and high-conflict divorce; has been teaching other custody evaluators, attorneys, and judges on these issues; and has reviewed over 200 reports of her peers. Her most recent book was co-written with Dr. David Frick on consulting with attorneys in forensic matters.

or negatively about the other parent; and flexibility or rigidity in parenting time issues. Most of this was simply not assessed. Dr. Nolan only focused on the mother's unwillingness to force Jane to see her father, rather than exploring this issue in sufficient depth as it related to both parents.

- Dr. Nolan didn't sufficiently explore why father appears to be allowing Joey to call Ms. Starks "Mom."
- Dr. Nolan did not explain the basis for the conclusion that children cannot have shared parenting with each parent just because of poor communication and high conflict between parents. This is especially true when both parents have a history of generally quite good parenting skills. Additionally, the evaluator recommended either a parenting coordinator or co-parent counselor who could also help these parties achieve a successful shared parenting plan.
- Parenting quality/skills was another area explored with limited depth. Dr. Nolan did not sufficiently assess how much the mother has been absenting herself in the children's lives since she began her new job.
- Another area with lack of depth is the assessment of the history of conflict between the mother and the father. The report implies that the conflicts started when the mother went back to work, and even suggests that the father is the cause of the conflicts. It is evident that Dr. Nolan simply did not assess this history and the causes of current conflicts sufficiently.

Other items of note:

- Dr. Nolan did an insufficient assessment of Joey's intermittent bedwetting and increased school challenges.
- There is inadequate explanation why Dr. Nolan believes in forcing Jane to be with her father. This needs to be better understood, as it appears to be a significant factor in Dr. Nolan's conclusions and recommendations.
- Dr. Nolan's explanation as to why no psychological testing was included in the evaluation seems appropriate. but psychological testing might have uncovered unknown problems and indicated the extent to which either parent was more inclined to respond to the evaluation with socially desirable answers rather than speaking more open and honestly.
- Given Dr. Henne's concerns about the weight loss and Jane's increased refusal to spend time with her father, it might have been helpful for Jane to have a more comprehensive evaluation.

Critical trial/deposition suggestions, especially since you are likely doing direct examination of Dr. Nolan:

- It's always better to get things out in direct that might be used by the other side against you. The other side will likely suggest that Dr. Nolan is biased against the mother—perhaps related to the article about the father's rights and maternal gatekeeping. You might want to explore that first, to show the court that, despite that article, Dr. Nolan approached this assessment in a comprehensive, neutral, and unbiased manner.

- Elicit Dr. Nolan's understanding of different types of gatekeeping and how this was explored in more depth than the report shows (see comment on this subject above). It's important to note that Dr. Nolan was in a workshop I conducted for custody evaluators and attorneys on the topic of gatekeeping in January of this year. At that workshop, gatekeeping was discussed in depth, and Dr. Nolan is likely to be able to explain based on what was covered there.
- Encourage Dr. Nolan to provide research support for the various conclusions and recommendations.
- Consider asking Dr. Nolan about the father's apparent narcissism—was it considered, and why does it not rise above the concerns regarding the mother and her restrictive gatekeeping and anger toward the father? It is likely that the other side will try and use that against Dr. Nolan (and your client). A simple definition of narcissism is the pursuit of gratification from *vanity* or *egotistic* admiration of one's own attributes. Dr. Allen displays such tendencies. But be aware that narcissism has both positive and negative elements. For someone to be a physician and having gone to medical school and succeeded is a form of positive narcissism. Negative elements of narcissism include lack of empathy, a tendency to personalize, and a tendency to view oneself as superior to others.

I hope all of these points are helpful in your analysis and examination of Dr. Nolan. As always, if you have any questions, please do not hesitate to contact me. Thank you for allowing me to be of assistance to you in this matter.

Sincerely,

Judy Frack

Dr. Judy Frack

Confidential Materials for Respondent's Counsel

Memorandum

To: *Allen v. Allen* file
From: Counsel
Re: Summary of background facts

This memorandum summarizes the background facts of *Allen* v. *Allen* as learned from our client and review of documents supplied by our client. It includes observations of counsel.

The Allen's Marriage and Children

In the summer of YR-16, about seven months after his relationship with a nurse ended, David Allen met Lynne Grant, who was a patient representative. They began meeting for coffee to discuss the progress of his patients. The conversations soon turned to more general discussions of medicine and of David's interest in developing a radiology practice after finishing his residency. Lynne was very attracted to David, who seemed very intelligent and confident about the future. They would spend long hours going over his research results. Lynne helped edit his research reports and also helped write and edit his first published article.

In the fall of YR-16, David asked Lynne to marry him. He said that since his career seemed to be going very well, he was ready to settle down. Lynne and David married on February 2, YR-15. When they married, both David and Lynne assumed they would have children. David felt that they should begin their family only when they were on secure financial footing.

In the summer of YR-14, David finished his residency and fellowship. He decided to open a private radiology practice. Lynne helped him plan the practice in detail and provided emotional support for his future plans. She helped design the office space and hire staff. She also entertained at dinners for potential referral sources such as hospital administrators and other doctors. The practice flourished.

David and Lynne decided they were financially secure enough to begin their family. Their first child, Jane, was born in YR-13. In YR-11, a second child, Joey, was born. Lynne agreed to stay home with the children until they reached school age. Lynne says she did this somewhat reluctantly, as she feared the social isolation and lack of adult and community contact that might result from staying at home full time. However, she found great satisfaction in motherhood and became active in the community.

By YR-10, with Jane approaching preschool and Joey about to start toddling, Lynne and David decided to leave their Nita City apartment and move to the suburbs. They purchased a large older home in Huntington, Nita (an attractive suburb), close to where David's parents lived, which Lynne began fixing up.

Lynne Allen's Return to School and Entrance into the Workforce

By YR-6, with Joey in kindergarten, Lynne felt she wanted to complete her degree and return to the working world. Lynne transferred her Bennington credits to Nita University, where she could commute to classes and complete her BA on a part-time basis. She changed her major to communications, and through her course work she became involved in programming at WNUR, the campus radio station.

In YR-4, Lynne received her BA in communications. Through her community activities, she became friends with a woman who sold advertising time on a twenty-four-hour news format radio station. Lynne's friend put her in touch with several people in management at local radio stations. Lynne's networking eventually produced an offer from a small commercial station that she admired, WKJW, whose studios are near Nita University. The station featured a mixed bag of information and music, appealing to upwardly mobile, middle-class tastes. Lynne accepted a part-time position with the station in the programming and feature development department.

David seemed pleased that Lynne had completed her college degree. According to Lynne, he did, however, express some ambivalence to her about her return to work. While he said he understood her desire to reestablish an identity separate from wife and mother and to prepare for the inevitable day when Jane and Joey grew up, he worried what effect it would have on the children.

Once Lynne started working, David repeatedly said she became much less supportive of him and his work. In the evening, after the children were in bed, he said that she was often more interested in catching up on her paperwork and discussing programming ideas with him than in sharing the ups and downs of his practice. David felt Lynne seemed to be focusing more energy and attention on work and less on Jane and Joey. Lynne recognized David's concerns and feelings about her career but felt he would eventually adjust.

Lynne said David had always been an active parent to his children, taking them on outings and supervising their homework. As a doctor, David took responsibility for the children's medical care. Before going to work at the radio station, Lynne was responsible for such things as cooking meals, feeding and bathing the children, putting them to bed, and getting up with them in the night. When Lynne started working, David seems to have adjusted his schedule and became more involved with the day-to-day care of the children, spending more of his evenings with Jane and Joey and fewer evenings with his journals and practice development details.

Despite David's claims, Lynne says she continued to devote a substantial amount of time and energy to caring for the children. She was insistent that they not be "shortchanged" by her return to work. She found her new schedule left her frazzled, with less time than she liked for interests other than her work and her children. Lynne, however, felt invigorated by her job. She found she had a keen sense for radio work and earned increasing responsibility at the station. She told David that she felt she had given her "all" to her family for thirteen years and was now ready to grow in other ways.

In the fall of YR-3, Lynne accepted a full-time position as assistant programming director of WKJW. Her programming duties expanded, and she now had control of "new feature" development. The salary—$30,000—was small for the position, but Lynne felt that she would miss a rare opportunity to gain experience should she pass it up.

The Deterioration of the Allen's Marriage

David told Lynne that he felt she was barely managing to have time for her work and the children. Their relationship was left completely out of the equation. Lynne says communications between her and David were limited. Their previously active sex life deteriorated dramatically. David made statements that could be interpreted as showing signs that he resented Lynne's career, while Lynne felt his resentment was unreasonable. David told Lynne she was becoming withdrawn and avoided discussing their marital problems. In Lynne's view David was yelling at her. Lynne told David he didn't take her feelings or her career seriously. David seems to have responded by becoming even angrier, saying he didn't know what Lynne's feelings were since she never discussed them.

Three years ago, further strain was placed on the Allen's marriage when Lynne was promoted to full-time assistant programming director. David's comments, far from easing the tension, made Lynne increasingly angry.

On a number of occasions in late YR-3, Lynne called David at work, saying that he needed to take care of Jane and Joey so that she could work late at the station. David seemed to resent having to leave his practice responsibilities to take care of the children. Twice, Lynne arrived home very late with alcohol on her breath. David seemed very upset and alarmed since previously Lynne rarely drank (which Lynne confirmed). She told David that she had merely had a drink with dinner to relax (Exhibit 5).

During one particularly heated argument with Lynne in January YR-2, David told Lynne that he was having an affair with Norma Starks, his x-ray technician. He announced he wanted a divorce, so he could continue his involvement openly. After David admitted his affair to Lynne, he left the marital residence and stayed with Norma in her apartment in Nita City.

This living arrangement continued for about a month. David moved back into the marital residence, where he currently lives with Lynne and the children. David told Lynne he moved back in because he didn't want their marital difficulties to harm his relationship with the children, a harm he feared would be compounded if he lived out of the house. Lynne thinks he moved back because his lawyer thought he would help his legal claim to the children. David sleeps in the guest bedroom in the house, and Lynne sleeps in the bedroom they once shared. David spends several nights each week at Norma's apartment. The children know their parents are having marital problems and have overheard them arguing. There is no history of domestic violence between David and Lynne.

The Effect of Marital Problems on the Allen Children

David rejected Lynne's suggestions they go to counseling, saying that their relationship is over. Lynne told David she is in therapy, meeting weekly with a psychologist whose office is near her station. She said the focus of her therapy is an attempt to work out the tension she feels between balancing career concerns and family responsibilities.

Lynne also periodically suggests that David move out again. David continues to refuse these requests.

Jane and Joey spend Wednesday evenings and every other weekend with David. David tries to spend this time with Jane, but she refuses to participate in any activities with him. The parties agreed to this temporary parenting schedule.

The children are not doing well. Lynne says that daughter Jane has always been a bright, but head-strong girl. In past years when her parents' relationship seemed stable, she was intensely interested in school and friends. She was close to both parents.

Recently, Jane has become critical of her teachers and peers. She is actively involved in gymnastics, and her teachers and David became alarmed when she placed herself on a strict diet and began losing weight. Over the past three months she has lost nearly fifteen pounds. Jane is now 5′1″ and has lost sufficient weight to be 102 pounds. There is some concern she is exhibiting signs of an eating disorder.

Lynne thinks she is not in danger, and that her weight loss is normal for a child interested in gymnastics. In any event, Jane's pediatrician is monitoring the situation and has not expressed alarm.

Lynne feels that David is making a big problem out of Jane's weight when all the weight loss signifies is Jane's interest and participation in gymnastics. The doctor has never told Lynne that Jane's weight loss is an eating disorder, only that it should be monitored. Lynne thinks that Jane's weight is a reflection of a very athletic girl and looks good on her. (Exhibit 4).

Jane has stopped inviting friends home. Jane is very close to Lynne, and she vocally blames her father for her parents' marital difficulties and refuses to spend any time with him. She has repeatedly told the family that she intends to live with Lynne no matter what happens.

Joey, according to Lynne, is a rather shy but self-confident boy who does extremely well in school and has many friends. He usually admires his older sister. In the past he has identified with her attitudes. With the onset of the marital problems in the Allen household, Joey has come into increasing conflict with Jane. When Jane blames their father for the problems, Joey quarrels with her, saying Lynne is to blame or that both are to blame. Joey complains frequently about Lynne being away at work in the evenings. Joey insists that if David moves away again, he wants to move away with him. Joey also is now having great difficulty sleeping—often waking with nightmares—and he has wet the bed several times in recent months.

The children have told Lynne they met Norma and her children on several occasions. Jane had a significant negative reaction to Norma and does not want to spend time with her. Lynne raised Jane's reluctance to be with him while Norma is around with Jane. Jane reluctantly told Lynne about a conversation with Norma that greatly upset Jane. According to Jane, Norma recently told Jane and Joey they should "think of me as a second mother" and "feel free to call me 'Mom.'" Jane told Lynne that Norma offered to take her to the mall to buy clothes. Jane asked Lynne, "Mom, am I losing you?"

Lynne then asked Joey about this conversation. Joey confirmed that it occurred. He also said, however, that Norma was friendly, sweet, and "cool," and she seemed very interested in both him and Jane. He reported getting along well with Norma and her children.

Lynne raised this incident with David. David told Lynne that Jane's reaction was simply the result of her over-identification with Lynne. David explained to Lynne that after the divorce and his marriage to Norma, the children would indeed have two mothers. Lynne said she became furious at this statement and stomped out of the room. Since this initial discussion, the subject has not been raised again.

According to Lynne, David wants to eliminate her from the "family" and substitute Norma for her. That is in part why she reacted negatively to David's invitation to take Jane and Joey to the state baseball championships in upstate Nita where Norma's son Jim was playing. David invited Jane and Joey along "as a family" to "support" Jim at the last minute without considering Jane and Joey's pre-exisiting activities. Lynne responded with some anger and sarcasm to David's invitation. (Exhibit 6). Her anger towards David was also reflected in a Facebook post (Exhibit 7) which she now recognizes was "ill-advised."

David claims that Lynne does not encourage Jane and Joey to have a good relationship with him. She denies this, but states that she cannot force Jane to see David when Jane does not want to. She points to text messages in which she encourages Jane to spend time with David (Exhibit 4).

David and Lynne recently received a letter from Joey and Jane's school psychologist (Exhibit 1). The psychologist indicated the children's teachers expressed concern about the children's behavior, in particular Jane's belligerence towards her teachers, her weight loss, and her recent falling grades. The school's Academic Dean expressed similar concerns in a letter to David and Lynne (Exhibit 2), and Jane's most recent report card reflects that her school performance is declining (Exhibit 3). When David and Lynne then met with relevant school personnel this information was confirmed.

As a result, David and Lynne agreed that Jane should have tutoring. They could not agree, though, on therapy for the children. David wanted to refer the children to someone he claimed to be a well-qualified therapist but who is a colleague of David's at Nita Medical Center. The colleague will accept less than the going rate for therapy. David claims his medical insurance does not provide for substantial mental health coverage for the kids. Lynne, however, will not agree to the children having therapy with David's colleague because she feels he will encourage the children to side with David over Lynne. He is using the medical insurance coverage as an excuse.

Lynne Allen's Career

In February YR-2, Lynne presented the WKJW managing board with a new feature proposal for their 1:00 PM weekday slot. Lynne told David that the "time slot had been a thorn in the side of station management for some time, plagued by low ratings and declining advertising revenues"' Lynne proposed trying a sports program with a new angle. The show's pitch would be to "baseball widows"—women with husbands so obsessively involved with sports the wives feel "widowed" during the season. The program would cover college and pro ball, highlighting current action and providing background and education about the sport. Construction of features would be from a woman's perspective, in a slightly humorous vein.

The station accepted the proposal and suggested Lynne host the show. Lynne created the concept and possessed the requisite sports knowledge to be successful. While Lynne's father instilled in her his passion for baseball, taking her to many games in her youth, Lynne maintained her interest in sports throughout her adult life; though not as fervent as her father, she remained an active spectator. Lynne, David, and the children often attended the major-league Nita City Cubs games, and Lynne avidly reads books, articles, blogs, statistics, and other baseball information.

Baseball Widows has a Facebook page (Exhibit 7). The show had its broadcast debut as spring training commenced in YR-1. By late summer, the audience was at an all-time high for the time slot, with positive effects for WKJW's other programs as new listeners tuned in. Fourth quarter YR-1 advertising revenues for this previous difficult time slot showed so dramatic an increase that the large local stations noticed. Early this year, Lynne and WKJW received several offers to market *Baseball Widows* nationally. She is currently entering negotiations with several radio networks. This may be the major turning point in her radio career. She could receive a raise in the near future and be making upwards of $50,000 a year.

Lynne has tried to meet important "players" in the radio industry. David regularly complains that Lynne comes home from business dinner with alcohol on her breath. Lynne informed him that a couple of drinks over dinner is a routine part of her business dinners (Exhibit 5). David also complains that Lynne has regularly asked him to rearrange his busy work schedule to take care of the children on very short notice (Exhibit 5). Lynne feels that she rarely asks for David to do so, and when she does it is for important business reasons. She spent a good deal of effort supporting David's career and she feels he "owes her" similar treatment now that she has a thriving career.

Current Relationship

Lynne has had a sexual relationship and began an affair with James Porter, a radio executive. They meet for dinner and go to his apartment approximately weekly. She intitially did not tell David about the affair and is sure the children do not know about it either. Lynne, however, did post about her relationship with James on Facebook recently (Exhibit 8) and suspects that David knows about it even though they haven't discussed it. James seems to want the relationship to become more serious, but Lynne is ambivalent. At present, Lynne has no plans to change the nature of her relationship with James.

Initiation of Litigation

Before initiating divorce litigation, David told Lynne that he felt he had to do so because they were not making substantial progress towards resolution. He told her that she was turning Jane against him. She told him to do what he felt he had to do, and that she would secure counsel to represent her interests. She then retained us.

Lynne was served with a complaint for divorce and associated relief on March 21, YR-1. We filed and served an answer and counterclaim on her behalf on May 4, YR-1.

Memorandum

To: *Allen v. Allen* file
From: Counsel
Re: Summary of Ms. Allen's views on parenting dispute

This memorandum summarizes Lynne's current thoughts on possible parenting plans for Joey, age ten, and Jane, age thirteen, in anticipation of settlement negotiations and mediation.

Shortly after Dr. Allen's complaint and Ms. Allen's counterclaim for divorce were filed and served they agreed to a parenting schedule by agreement. Jane and Joey are with David every other weekend and on Wednesday. David told Lynne repeatedly that this schedule does not give him adequate time with Jane and Joey. He told her he agreed to it to avoid a premature court hearing that would put the children in the middle.

David complains, however, that the situation has become intolerable. He claims that Lynne is encouraging Jane not to have anything to do with him. He continues to pressure Lynne to send the children to his colleague for therapy, and to accuse Lynne of being insufficiently concerned about Jane's weight loss. Lynne rejects his claims. She feels that Jane's weight loss is normal for a young girl interested in becoming a competitive gymnast, and says she cannot force Jane to visit with David if she does not want to.

Lynne wants to be the primary decision maker for the children and have the children spend the majority of the time with her. Lynne believes that Norma and David have caused the problems in the Allens's marriage. She is especially concerned that David is trying to replace her with Norma as the primary emotional attachment and caretaker in her children's lives.

Lynne is willing to agree to a parenting plan that involves David in Jane and Joey's lives. She does not want David's girlfriend to replace her as the children's mother, nor does she want the children to be forced against their will to have a relationship with David.

Lynne is opposed to joint parenting decision-making because she believes that David and Norma will use their power over Jane and Joey to shut Lynne out and replace her with Norma in the children's lives.

Lynne thinks that Jane's reaction to Norma's interference in her parents' marriage is normal. If David wants to develop a better relationship with Jane, he should simply give up Norma. If David is unwilling to give up Norma, Lynne wants him to move out of the house immediately and into his own apartment.

Lynne is worried about how Jane and Joey are dealing with the situation. She does think that David is overreacting to Jane's weight loss; she believes Jane looks better without all of the baby fat she has had since she was little. She is willing to consider sending the children to a neutral therapist if David will pay the cost. She is reluctant to have them enter therapy with David's colleague because she feels like he will take the opportunity to get the children to side with David if there is a residence battle.

If David wants to go to family therapy, Lynne will consider it, but she does not want Norma to be there, and she does not want to force the children if they do not want to go. Lynne also wants there to be restrictions on Norma's relationship with the children. She believes the children are confused and pressured enough without adding a third party to the mix.

Lynne would like to remain in the marital home with the children. She thinks this would be best for them so that they do not have to change schools.

DR. DAVID FRICK'S REPORT
EVALUATING DR. PAT NOLAN'S PARENTING EVALUATION
(FOR LYNNE ALLEN'S COUNSEL ONLY)

ATTORNEY WORK PRODUCT

Dr. David Frick[*]

June 1, YR-0

Victoria Fetterman
Nita Bar Building, Suite 222
Nita City, Nita 09999

Memo: Summary of concerns regarding Dr. Nolan's report from Consultant

Dear Ms. Fetterman:

I am writing this memo as your confidential consultant, hired to share my observations of the strengths and weaknesses of Dr. Nolan's report in the Allen matter in anticipation of Dr. Nolan's deposition and testimony at trial. As we discussed, I will not testify at trial.

In order of importance, here are what I see as the strengths of Dr. Nolan's report (please note the strengths will also have some weaknesses associated as well):

- Dr. Nolan utilized a multi-method process, conducting multiple interviews with the parties, interviewing the children, observing the children and each of their parents, reviewing collateral information, speaking with collateral witnesses, and writing a report focusing on the statutory factors.
- Dr. Nolan provided an analysis identifying risks/benefits of various custodial options.
- Dr. Nolan's approaches and procedures generally seemed balanced.

In order of importance, here are what I see as the weaknesses of Dr. Nolan's report:

- There is a general lack of depth in much of Dr. Nolan's assessment, which increases the risks that Dr. Nolan's conclusions are speculative and of limited usefulness.
- Seems biased against the mother—perhaps this is related to Dr. Nolan's article about father's rights and maternal gatekeeping. In this context, this is a very poor assessment of and analysis of each parent's respective gatekeeping behaviors. Gatekeeping occurs along a continuum and has multiple dimensions, including support of the child's relationship with the other parent (or lack thereof); qualities of communication (or problems in such); extent to which the parent encourages input on major decision-making (or marginalizes the other parent); extent to which the parent speaks positively or negatively about

[*] Dr. Frick is a licensed psychologist in the State of Nita who has been a forensic psychologist for nearly thirty years. He has conducted nearly 750 custody evaluations by court appointment; has written extensively on child custody matters and high-conflict divorce; has been teaching other custody evaluators, attorneys, and judges on these issues; and has reviewed over 200 reports of his peers. His most recent book was co-written with Dr. Judy Frack on consulting with attorneys in forensic matters.

the other parent; and flexibility or rigidity in parenting time issues. Most of this was simply not assessed. The report only focused on the mother's unwillingness to force Jane to see her father, rather than exploring this issue in sufficient depth.

- Also, Dr. Nolan's report seemed to minimize the extent to which the father appears to be allowing Ms. Starks to usurp the mother's role, at least by allowing Joey to call Ms. Starks "Mom." In fact, it is likely that each parent has a range of restrictive and facilitative gatekeeping behaviors, rather than just the mother's reluctance to force Jane's time with her father.
- Given the issues of gatekeeping that were not explored, it is impossible to determine if Dr. Nolan's primary reason for more time with father—i.e., the mother's apparent unwillingness to force Jane to see her father—should be given the highest priority.
- There is limited research to support the idea that children cannot have shared parenting with each parent just because of poor communication and high conflict between parents. This is especially true when both parents have a history of generally quite good parenting skills. Additionally, the evaluator recommended either a parenting coordinator or co-parent counselor who also could help these parties achieve a successful shared parenting plan.
- Parenting quality/skills was another area explored with limited depth. Dr. Nolan seemed to completely ignore the history of the mother being by far the primary parent in these children's lives and the likely closer bond that the children, especially Jane, have with her.
- Another area with lack of depth is the assessment of the history of conflict between the mother and father. It appears from the report that the conflicts only began when the mother decided to go back to work, combined with the father's frustration with this. The history of conflict needed to be explored more thoroughly.
- Dr. Nolan notes the father's tendencies to be narcissistic but seemed to give it minimal weight, despite the fact that the father is now blaming the mother because she went back to work, and despite the fact he was a much more absent parent earlier in the children's lives.
- Given the issues noted as weaknesses, it is likely that psychological testing of the parents could have been helpful and provided some insight into psychological issues contributing to their conflict and other aspects of their case. Psychological testing could be important because it might give more insight into the extent of the father's narcissistic tendencies.
- It appears as if the father is more focused on relationship with his girlfriend than focusing on the kids. The father not in tune with kids' experience of the divorce. All of this, along with allowing Joey to call Ms. Starks "Mom" suggests he may be trying to supplant the mother, and also it suggests that the father may not be as supportive of kids being involved with their mother as he states.
- Did Dr. Nolan consider the hypothesis that the father is bright and knows what to say? Psychological testing can also suggest if the father might have been faking good answers and trying to present himself in a favorable light.

Other items of note:

- It is unclear to what extent Dr. Nolan has sufficient understanding of the children's issues. There is minimal exploration of Jane's weight loss issues, Joey's intermittent bedwetting, and Joey's increased school challenges.
- Forcing Jane to live with the father could create more problems. While she needs to improve her relationship with her father, it could cause significant emotional harm to force a child who won't see her father to suddenly have to live with him. This is unlikely to be in her best psychological interest and might also contribute to further weight loss.
- Dr. Nolan states the mother did well as primary caregiver and did a "very effective job." The children did well. Thus, why change it?
- Dr. Nolan has no clear evidence of eating difficulties, per the pediatrician, yet, even writing as a psychologist and not a physician, Dr. Nolan says the mother has little insight into Jane's eating difficulties. As with many of these issues being described, Dr. Nolan provides no basis for these conclusions.

Regarding deposition and/or trial, as you will likely be cross-examining Dr. Nolan, I would suggest the following:

- Explore the limited depth of assessment of gatekeeping, parenting history and parenting quality, and history of conflict.
- Explore the basis for each of Dr. Nolan's conclusions in this matter, especially Dr. Nolan's apparent conclusions that the mother does not understand Jane's weight loss issues, that the father is more supportive of mother's relationship with the children than vice versa, and that it is not in the children's best interests to remain in the mother's primary (or shared) custody.
- Explore what multiple hypotheses Dr. Nolan considered regarding Jane's anger at and refusal to spend time with her father, rather than just the one hypothesis regarding the mother's lack of support. The father's extramarital affair alone is sufficient to plausibly cause Jane to be angry with her father and decline to spend time with him.
- Also, use your constructive cross to elicit the strengths of mother's parenting history, the fact that the children did quite well while in her primary care and before the conflicts started, and the appropriateness of mother seeking employment outside the house and father's inappropriate negative judgment of this.

I hope all of these points are helpful in your analysis and cross-examination of Dr. Nolan. As always, if you have any questions, please do not hesitate to contact me. Thank you for allowing me to be of assistance to you in this matter.

Sincerely,

David Frick

Dr. David Frick

Valuation Dispute Materials

Materials Available to All Counsel

BACKGROUND FOR DEPOSITIONS ON THE EQUITABLE DISTRIBUTION/VALUATION DISPUTE

(Both parties have the same information.)

I. Overview of Equitable Distribution

Dr. Allen, a radiologist, began his practice fourteen years ago and the marital value of his practice is an asset that must be considered in the distribution of the parties' assets and liabilities. The distribution of the parties' assets and liabilities in a dissolution of marriage action is called equitable distribution.

In divorce actions, parties disclose their assets in certified financial statements. Based on these statements, there are generally three steps in determining equitable distribution of marital assets. First, the court determines (or the parties agree) about what property is included in the marital "pot." Next, the court determines the value of each asset. Finally, the court determines how the asset is distributed.

Nita statutes provide for equitable distribution of marital property.

- Marital property (as distinguished from separate property) is defined as all property of either or both spouses acquired during the marriage and before the execution of a separation agreement or commencement of an action for divorce, regardless of the form in which title to the property is held.

- Marital property can include intangible assets such as pension plans, stock options, and the accounts receivable of a business created during the marriage.

- Equitable distribution means that the court divides marital property fairly—not necessarily equally—based on a host of economic and noneconomic factors such as need of a spouse and contribution to the business, homemaking services, etc.

- Generally, what the "pot" of marital property includes, and the value of marital property, is determined as of the date an action for divorce is commenced in court. Subsequent events, such as the amount of accounts receivable actually collected between the date of commencement of the divorce action and the date of trial, are not considered in the valuation of the accounts receivable.

II. The Background of the Upcoming Depositions on Valuation Issues

The depositions of the valuation experts take place after the depositions of David and Lynne Allen (relevant excerpts follow) and after significant negotiations between counsel about equitable distribution of the Allen's marital property:

- The parties have stipulated that the accounts receivable of Dr. Allen's medical practice are marital property subject to equitable distribution.

- The parties have agreed on the value of all other marital property, except the value of the accounts receivable of Dr. Allen's medical practice. The parties have also agreed that the marital property should be divided equally. A table follows which shows what agreements the parties have made so far to distribute marital property.

- The parties would have submitted more papers to the court and each other in connection with determining the valuation of marital property, child support, and maintenance. The papers submitted would have included detailed financial statements showing assets and liabilities and budgets. The experts who submitted reports on the valuation of the accounts receivable might (or might not) have considered that material in creating their reports. That material is not, however, provided in the case file because of its marginal relevance and to avoid making the dispute over valuation of accounts receivable more difficult to understand.

III. Expert Reports on the Valuation of the Accounts Receivable

As the parties were not able to settle the valuation of the accounts receivable, each side has retained its own financial expert to assist with the valuation of the practice. Each expert has produced a report on the valuation of the accounts receivable that has been disclosed to the other side pursuant to discovery rules. Both reports have been exchanged by counsel for Dr. Allen and Ms. Allen. Both experts have been designated as testifying experts for trial.

Accounts receivable in relation to a medical practice refers to outstanding payments owed to the practice by its patients. Accounts receivable owed to the practice is the largest asset of Dr. Allen's practice, and as such, the value of it will make a substantial difference in the overall distribution of the parties' total marital net worth. All of the other assets and liabilities of the parties have been agreed upon.

Dr. Allen's expert is a Certified Public Accountant and has the designation as a Certified Business Appraiser by a nationally recognized association.

Ms. Allen's expert is a college professor of finance with expertise in business consulting specifically to medical practices.

There are three main methods used by business valuators in order to value a business: the asset approach, the income approach, and market approach. The relevant method of valuation for Dr. Allen's practice is an asset-based approach, which focuses on the company's net asset value—i.e., the assets of the business minus its liabilities. Financial statements are properly prepared for Dr. Allen's business, including a balance sheet that details his assets and liabilities at historical cost. However, to quantify the value of the practice, certain adjustments must be made.

Dr. Allen's practice uses the "cash basis" accounting method, which reports income when it is received; expenses are reported when they are paid. The cash basis methodology is used by many doctors' offices because patients may only pay their co-pay on the date of their appointment and the remainder owed must be collected by third-party insurance.

The uncollected amounts for services that were performed but for which payment has not been received is called accounts receivable. Most of the payments for services by a physician are not received until months after the services are performed. While the financial statements of the practice may not include the outstanding receivable balance, medical practices normally maintain their accounts receivable records in specialized computer accounting systems or hire outside billing specialists to maintain and collect these receivables.

Unique to the medical profession is the influence of government programs such as Medicaid, Medicare, etc., and medical insurance policies. These third-party payors have such influence that they established a wholesale pricing schedule for covered medical procedures. However, for non-covered medical procedures, physicians and hospitals establish a higher retail pricing for services. These higher retail rates are also applied to patients who chose to obtain services from a physician who has not contracted with an individuals's health insurance company. Consequently, estimating the collectible value of accounts receivable is challenging. Only the collections realized over the passage of time would accurately determine the value of a specific date. Payments received from insurance companies or government entities are referred to as reimbursement payments.

The amount of reimbursement payments varies for each type of service, by each insurance company or government, and geographic location. Determining the collectible value of accounts receivable (i.e., unpaid services) at a specific date requires some quantification.

The two experts agree that the accounts receivable balance as of date of filing is $1,200,000, but they differ on the expectation of how much of the receivables will actually be collected by the medical practice. Of the $1,200,000 owed, $300,000 is over 120 days old. The experts agree that the past due amount older than 120 days are only collectible at a rate of 20 percent, and therefore the value is only $60,000.

Dr. Allen's expert, Cecilia Price, CPA, ABV, indicates that the collectible value of the remainder of the $900,000 Accounts Receivable (less than 120 days old) is 40 percent, at $360,000. Ms. Price analyzed the collection of accounts receivable by the practice over the last three years and applied the average of this collection rate to the receivables owed as of date of filing. Ms. Price also considered that the accounts receivable would have been subject to income taxes had they been collected by the valuation date, and therefore she applied a 25 percent income tax rate. Ms. Price used the 25 percent income tax rate because it is the combined average tax rate for federal and Nita taxes. In addition, Ms. Price discounted the receivables at a rate of 10 percent because soon after the date of filing of the dissolution of marriage, Dr. Allen lost one of his employees who handled the collections of accounts receivable for the practice. The new person hired for collections was still going through training.

Over 120 days past due amounts	$60,000
Under 120 days past due amounts	$360,000
Total gross amount	$420,000
Less 10% discount due to staff turnover	($42,000)
Net Value of accounts receivable before taxes	$378,000
Less taxes estimated at 25%	($94,500)
Net value of accounts receivable after taxes	**$283,500**

Ms. Allen's expert, John Ernst PhD, reaches a different conclusion. Based on his extensive medical practice consulting work and his comparison of other collectability rates of other radiology practices located outside of Nita, he concluded that the remaining $900,000 of accounts receivable would be 70 percent collectible. He also considered that the accounts receivable would have been subject to income taxes had they been collected by the valuation date and applied a 25 percent income tax rate.

Over 120 days past due amounts	$60,000
Under 120 days past due amounts	$630,000
Net value of accounts receivable before taxes	$690,000
less taxes estimated at 25%	($172,500)
Net value of accounts receivable after taxes	**$517,500**

The following chart summarizes what the parties have agreed on and what disputed items remain.

	Distribution of Assets/Liabilities		
Asset/Liability	**Agreed-Upon Value**	**Dr. Allen**	**Ms. Allen**
AGREED-UPON ITEMS:			
Cash in accounts (marital)	$20,000	$10,000	$10,000
Investments (marital)	$125,000		$125,000
Marital home (equity)	$380,000		$380,000
Dr. Allen's vehicle	$20,000	$20,000	
Ms. Allen's vehicle	$15,000		$15,000
Dr. Allen's 401(k) IRA (after-tax value) *	$300,000	$300,000	
Ms. Allen's Roth IRA (after-tax funds)	$15,000		$15,000
Life insurance (term)	No cash value		
Credit cards (marital)	($10,000)	($10,000)	
Practice value (including equity in office condo and other assets, but not including accounts receivable)	$225,000	$225,000	
SUBTOTAL	**$1,090,000**	**$545,000**	**$545,000**
DISPUTED ITEMS (*Note*: Dr. Allen will owe Ms. Allen half of the accounts receivable value agreed upon by the parties. Dr. Allen's value is $283,500, and Ms. Allen's value is $517,500.):	?	?	?
TOTAL			

** Dr. Allen can access funds to pay Ms. Allen for her 50 percent share of accounts receivable by taking a loan of up to $280,000 against his 401(k).*

STIPULATIONS FOR VALUATION DEPOSITIONS

On Governing Law

- Nita statutes provide for equitable distribution of marital property.
  - Marital property (as distinguished from separate property) is defined as all property of either or both spouses acquired during the marriage and before the execution of a separation agreement or commencement of an action for divorce, regardless of the form in which title to the property is held.
  - Marital property can include such intangible assets as pension plans, stock options, and the accounts receivable of a business created during the marriage.
  - Equitable distribution means that the court divides marital property fairly—not necessarily equally—based on a host of economic and non-economic factors such as need of a spouse and contribution to the business, homemaking services, etc.
  - What the "pot" of marital property includes, and the value of marital property, is determined as of the date an action for divorce is commenced in court. Subsequent events such as the amount of accounts receivable actually collected between the date of commencement of the divorce action and the date of trial are not considered in the valuation of the accounts receivable.

On the Scope of the Dispute

- The parties have stipulated that the accounts receivable of Dr. Allen's medical practice are marital property subject to equitable distribution.
- The parties have agreed on the equitable distribution of all other marital property, except the value of the accounts receivable of Dr. Allen's medical practice.

On the Reports

- Both experts have used different methodologies and believe the other expert has made errors.
- Accounts receivable collectability can be affected by the location of the practice.
- The income tax adjustment is appropriate due to the facts that the practice reports on a cash basis and tax is not paid on receivables until received.

On the Procedure

- Both experts have been designated as testifying experts for trial.
- Both experts prepared reports describing their valuation and methodology, which have been exchanged.
- The parties have also exchanged résumés of their testifying experts.

- Both experts have provided their counsel with comments on the other expert's report that, for purposes of discovery and trial, is protected work product.
- The parties would have submitted more papers to the court and one another in connection with determining equitable distribution of marital property, child support, and maintenance. The papers submitted would have included detailed financial statements and budgets. The experts who submitted reports on the valuation of the accounts receivable might (or might not) have considered that material in creating their reports. That material is not, however, provided in the case file because of its marginal relevance and to avoid making the dispute over valuation of accounts receivable more difficult to understand. No questions can be asked of a witness based on the absence of financial affidavits, etc.

Excerpt from Deposition of Dr. David Allen

An excerpt from the deposition of Dr. David Allen taken on July 12, YR-0, by counsel for Lynne Allen follows.

Q: Describe Lynne's role in the development of your medical practice.

A: She was a lot of help before she went back to school to get her degree. She functioned as a kind of unofficial "office manager." She knew the personnel I had in the office well and often made suggestions for improving office procedure such as on collections for past due accounts. She helped design the office and order office furniture.

Q: What happened when Lynne went back to school?

A: She stopped paying attention to anything at the office. All she focused on was her career. She stopped calling the people who worked for me, visiting the office, or asking me anything about what was going on. She stopped making suggestions for improving office procedures. She didn't even come to the annual office party. I doubt she knows who was working for the practice or what they were doing.

Excerpt from Deposition of Lynne Allen

An excerpt from the deposition of Lynne Allen taken on July 13, YR-0, by counsel for Dr. David Allen follows.

Q: Describe your role in the development of Dr. Allen's medical practice.

A: I helped him plan and develop it. I helped make plans for office design and talked to him constantly about office procedures and practices. We talked about how to improve his collections of accounts receivable, which were always a problem area. I helped him hire and evaluate personnel. I entertained doctors who were possible referral sources. David once introduced me to another doctor as his "unofficial office manager."

Q: How did your involvement in Dr. Allen's medical practice change after you went back to school and began to pursue a career in communications?

A: I admit I was less focused on developing the medical practice and more on developing my own career. I did try hard, though, to help David through any crisis that he encountered. After all, his practice supported me, too. I don't think much has changed in David's practice in recent years. But after a time, all the yelling and screaming between us discouraged me from talking to him about anything.

Report of Cecilia Price (Dr. David Allen's Valuation Expert)

Cecilia Price, CPA, ABV
111 Cheap Street
Nita City, Nita 09999

August 1, YR-0

To Whom It May Concern:

Dr. Allen asked me to value the accounts receivables for his practice as of the date of filing of the divorce between Dr. and Ms. Allen. I have a been practicing as a CPA for over twenty years and am licensed in the State of Nita. I also regularly assist with the compilation of the practice financial statements and complete the required IRS filings for the practice, including the completion of the annual corporate practice tax return. I have not performed any accounting services for Dr. and Ms. Allen outside my role as the accountant for Dr. Allen's medical practice. I do not prepare the personal tax returns for the parties.

My practice includes general accounting and tax preparation, business consulting, and business valuation services. My clients represent a broad array of professions and businesses.

Dr. Allen's practice revenues are recorded by his bookkeepers in QuickBooks, a software program that helps small businesses manage their accounting records. Each year, I review the QuickBooks accounting for the practice and assist with any questions or problems with data entry into QuickBooks. I also make any necessary year-end, adjusted journal entries.

On an annual basis, I have reviewed the accounts receivable of Dr. Allen's practice. The practice accounts receivable are categorized as follows: 1) private pay, 2) Medicare pay, 3) Medicaid pay, and 4) other insurance pay. Also on an annual basis, I conduct an analysis to determine how much of each type of accounts receivable is collected. Over the last three years, the percentage of receivables collected in each of the above accounts receivables categories has been consistent. Using the percentage collected from the most recent year analyzed (YR-1), the practice has collected, on average, 25 percent of private pay receivables (< 120 days), 20 percent of Medicare pay receivables (< 120 days), 15 percent of Medicaid Pay receivables (< 120 days), and 50 percent of other insurance pay receivables (< 120 days).

I then calculated the percentage of each type of accounts receivable that existed as of the date of filing in this action.

Determination of Percentage of Total Receivables

	Accounts receivable as of date of filing	Percentage of total receivables
Private Pay	$279,000	31%
Medicare Pay	$36,000	4%
Medicaid Pay	$36,000	4%
Other Insurance Pay	$549,000	61%
TOTAL	$900,000	100%

Finally, I applied the average percentages of receivable collection in YR-1 (broken down by receivable type) to the percentages of the receivables that existed as of date of filing in this matter.

Determination of Average Collectability Based on Collectability Percentages in YR-1 Applied to Existing Accounts Receivable as of Date of Filing

	YR-1 %	AR Type/Total AR (Date of Filing)	Weighted Applicable %
Private Pay	25%	31%	7.75%
Medicare Pay	20%	4%	0.80%
Medicaid Pay	15%	4%	0.60%
Other Insurance Pay	50%	61%	30.50%
	Average percentage of collectability		39.65%
	Average percentage of collectability rounded		40%
	Accounts receivable < 120 days		$900,000
	Total collectible accounts receivable < 120 days (rounded)		$360,000

Accounts Receivable over 120 days old has historically been collected at a 20 percent rate. My understanding is that Ms. Allen's financial expert also agrees with this rate. Thus, the $300,000 of accounts receivable that is over 120 days old is worth $60,000 ($300,000 x 20% = $60,000).

Two employees collected accounts receivable during the period analyzed. Just after the dissolution of action was filed, one of the employees responsible for collections resigned and Dr. Allen had to hire a replacement. This replacement lacks the experience level of the prior employee. I therefore have discounted the collection of accounts receivable by another 10 percent.

Finally, because Dr. Allen reports his income using the cash basis method of accounting, he does not record or pay taxes on accounts receivable until received. As such, I have applied a 25 percent tax rate on the total receivables that I conclude Dr. Allen will receive. The income tax rate of 25 percent is the combined average tax rate for federal and Nita taxes, based on the parties' YR-1 tax return.

While I do not have any other radiologists as clients, I am confident that Dr. Allen's billing procedures reflect the intent of the practice to maximize revenues. Dr. Allen has historically not pursued the most aggressive collection practices because of the fear of malpractice suits. I did not look at national averages in considering the collectability of Dr. Allen's accounts receivables because there was historical data by which to analyze Dr. Allen's actual collections. In addition, data in other regions may not compare to Dr. Allen's specific practice.

In conclusion, I have analyzed and calculated the fair market value of Dr. Allen's accounts receivable as of the date of filing in this matter by using the following methodology:

1) Accounts receivable over 120 days past due was valued as collectible at a 20 percent rate, based on historical collection rates.
2) Accounts receivable under 120 days old was valued as collectible at a 40 percent rate, using the last year of collectability of the relevant types of receivables in Dr. Allen's practice. I analyzed the last three years and found the collectability rates to be consistent.
3) Because of recent staff turnover in collections, I discounted collectible receivables by a 10 percent rate.
4) Finally, I taxed the affected collectible accounts receivable at a 25 percent rate because Dr. Allen reports on the cash basis method of accounting.

In conclusion, the total fair market value of Dr. Allen's accounts receivable as of the date of filing is as follows:

Over 120 days past-due amounts	$60,000
Under 120 days past-due amounts	$360,000
Total gross amount	$420,000
Less 10% discount due to staff turnover	($42,000)
Net value of accounts receivable before taxes	$378,000
Less taxes estimated at 25%	($94,500)
Net value of accounts receivable after taxes	**$283,500**

Finally, my hourly rate for litigation support and business valuation services is $250 per hour. I have expended thirty-five hours on my analyses of the valuation issues related to Dr. Allen's practice. My fees charged prior to date (not including the trial in this matter) are $8,750. These fees have been paid by Dr. Allen.

Sincerely,

Cecilia Price

Cecilia Price, CPA, ABV

Cecilia Price, CPA, ABV

POSITION

Managing Member, Price & Fields, LLC

EDUCATIONAL & PROFESSIONAL DESIGNATION

CPA, Certified Public Accountant, State of Nita, YR-21

ABV, Accredited in Business Valuation (American Institute of Certified Public Accountants), YR-15

BS, University of Michigan, YR-22

EXPERIENCE

Extensive experience with all aspects of tax, audit, review, compilation, and business advisory services; accredited and experienced in business valuation; qualified in multiple counties in Nita as an expert witness in family law and civil litigation.

PROFESSIONAL AFFILIATIONS

Member, American Institute of Certified Public Accountants

Member, Nita Institute of Certified Public Accountants

Member, AICPA Forensics and Valuation Services (FVS) Section

Member, Nita Business Advisory Counsel

Member, Nita County Bar Association—Associate Member

PROFESSIONAL HISTORY

Price & Fields, LLC

Managing Member, October YR-5

Tax Manager, Tax and Business Consultant, and Business Valuation Specialist

Founders and Principals, LLC

Tax and Business Consultant, August YR-20 to September YR-15

PROFESSIONAL EDUCATION

AICPA, National Business Valuation School, YR-3

FICPA, Valuation Forensic Accounting & Litigation Services Conference, YR-13, YR-9, and YR-6

AICPA, Forensic & Valuation Conference, YR-7, YR-2, and YR-1

NACVA, Expert Witness Training, YR-3

Family Mediation Certification Training, YR-6

Nita Family Law Section Trial Advocacy—Workshop, Expert Witness Volunteer, YR-5 to YR-1

REPORT OF JOHN ERNST, PHD (LYNNE ALLEN'S VALUATION EXPERT)

John Ernst, Ph.D.
999 Prosperous Street
Nita City, Nita 09998

August 4, YR-0

To Whom It May Concern:

Lynne Allen retained me to value the accounts receivable of the Allen practice. I have been a professor of finance at Nita University for the past five years, a frequent guest lecturer at University of South Nita, and have provided lectures at multiple continuing-education seminars for medical practices within the State of Nita. In addition, I provide consulting services for multiple businesses, including several radiology medical practices, with regards to their collection procedures. These practices are not located in Nita, but I believe that their practices are very similar to Dr. Allen's.

I have been provided with the QuickBooks information of Dr. Allen's practice by Dr. Allen and reviewed his accounts receivable. I have compared each category of pay with the experience of the three similar radiology practices to which I provide consulting services. The data I used in this comparison were obtained for the purposes of completing a research study regarding these practices for an article that I later published. I found that the three radiology practices collected, on the average, much more than Dr. Allen's practice over the three-year period that I analyzed for my study.

As such, if Dr. Allen followed the procedures used by these radiology practices, I believe that collections for accounts receivable (less than 120 days) should be 70 percent collectable. As such, I recommend valuing his receivables as follows:

	Collection Averages/ Other Practices	Related Date of Filing Accounts Receivable	Total Collectable
Private Pay	64%	$279,000	$178,560
Medicare Pay	78%	$36,000	$28,080
Medicaid Pay	78%	$36,000	$28,080
Other Insurance Pay	72%	$549,000	$395,280
	TOTAL	$900,000	$630,000
	Average Collectability		**70.00%**

Based on what Ms. Allen told me about the practice, I believe that the accounts receivable personnel working for Dr. Allen should be much more experienced and proactive in collecting patient revenue. Dr. Allen could improve on his collection of accounts receivable by having his staff making monthly phone calls to each party and following up on accounts receivable more frequently than monthly statements, if they are not already doing so. If necessary, additional training for Dr. Allen's employees could also yield a significant increase in collections.

The final adjustment necessary to determine the fair market value of Dr. Allen's accounts receivable as of the date of filing is the tax that Dr. Allen will have to pay as he collects these past due payments from patients. I have considered an average tax rate of 25 percent.

In conclusion, I have analyzed and calculated the fair market value of Dr. Allen's accounts receivable as of the date of filing in this matter in the following manner:

1) Accounts receivable over 120 days past due was valued as collectible at a 20 percent rate, based on historical collection rates.

2) Accounts receivable under 120 days old was valued at a 70 percent rate, using average collection data obtained by me in a study of three practices very similar to that of Dr. Allen's.

3) An average 25 percent tax rate was applied to the final collectable accounts receivable.

Thus, the total fair market value of Dr. Allen's accounts receivable as of the date of filing is as follows:

Over 120 days past-due amounts	$60,000
Under 120 days past-due amounts	$630,000
Net value of accounts receivable before taxes	$690,000
less taxes estimated at 25%	($172,500)
Net value of accounts receivable after taxes	**$517,500**

My hourly rate for consultant services including witness testimony is $275 an hour. I have expended thirty-eight hours on issues related to the valuation of the accounts receivable of Dr. Allen's practice. My total fee as of the date of this report is $10,450. I have not yet been paid as of today's date.

Sincerely,

John Ernst

John Ernst Ph.D.

John Ernst, PhD

APPOINTMENTS

Associate Professor, Finance Department, Nita University, YR-6 to present

Visiting Lecturer, University of South Nita, YR-14 to present

Associate Professor, Finance Department, Arizona State University, YR-12 to YR-6

Assistant Professor, Finance Department, Boston College, YR-19 to YR-12

POSITIONS

Business Consultant, John Ernst PhD, PA, YR-2 to present

Board of Directors, Bank of Nita, YR-7 to present

EDUCATIONAL & PROFESSIONAL DESIGNATION

PhD Finance from University of South Nita, YR-18

MS in Finance from Brown University, YR-20

EXPERIENCE

University professor for the finance field of study at multiple universities spanning a twenty-year period; lecturer for multiple professional business and other organizations; business consultant with experience working with clients on strategy planning, problem solving, and maximizing business profits.

PROFESSIONAL AFFILIATIONS

Member, Nita Business Advisory Council

Member, American Association of University Professors

Member, National Organization of Medical Practice Operations and Procedures

PUBLICATIONS

"How to Maximize Profits in Today's Medical Challenges," *Medical Press* (Oct. YR-1)

"Managing Financial Hurdles and Business Challenges," *Nita Times* (Jan. YR-2)

"How to Maximize Accounts Receivable Collectability of Medical Practices," *Harvard Business Review* (Sept. YR-3)

"Loopholes in Medicare Collections," *American Medical Association* (Nov. YR-4)

"Struggles of the Growing Medical Practice in Today's Medical Climate," *Medical Economics* (Sept. YR-12)

"Small Business Strategies for Medical Practices," *American Medical Association* (Nov. YR-16)

Confidential Analysis by Cecilia Price, CPA, ABV (Dr. David Allen's Valuation Expert)

Memo from Cecilia Price to Dr. Allen's Counsel, re John Ernst's Report and Potential Testimony

CONFIDENTIAL WORK PRODUCT

Issues Regarding the Report

- The practices analyzed by Dr. Ernst are not located in the same geographical area as Dr. Allen's. The collection of accounts receivable for a medical practice is very specific to that practice and the types of patients and insurance carriers they service.

- Dr. Ernst's study analyzed three practices for which he served as a consultant. Dr. Ernst would have required a fee for his services; therefore, there may have been some bias in the study.

- If a practice hires a business consultant such as Dr. Ernst to work with it regarding collectability (as is the case in the three practices he studied), then the medical practice would have had additional expenses relating to the consulting work. Dr. Ernst did not adjust the collectability of Dr. Allen's receivables for the additional cost related to hiring a consultant or implementing additional practice procedures over and above the current procedures that are currently expensed by the practice.

- The general rule in business valuation is only what is "known or knowable" as of the date of the valuation is considered. Historical collection procedures are known and knowable. The results of Dr. Ernst's suggested changes to collection procedures are not known and knowable. Even if the collection procedures Dr. Ernst suggested are put in place, it is not known or knowable whether they will be successful. Dr. Ernst's suggested outcome is speculative.

- Dr. Ernst suggested hiring more experienced personnel. More experienced personnel would cost more in salary, which Dr. Ernst did not adjust for.

- Dr. Ernst suggested that Dr. Allen could have his staff make more monthly phone calls. If Dr. Allen's staff is already working forty hours weekly and is already productive, additional staff would need to be hired. Dr. Ernst did not adjust for hiring additional staff.

- Dr. Ernst suggested additional training for employees regarding collections. This training would come at a cost, and Dr. Ernst did not adjust for this.

- Dr. Ernst suggested sending out additional monthly statements. Additional monthly statements would cost more in postage, paper, ink, and the time spent on creating the monthly statements. Dr. Ernst did not adjust for this.

- Dr. Ernst did not indicate if he interviewed or talked with Dr. Allen's staff. Does he have first-hand knowledge that the staff in place can handle the changes that he suggests? If not, how can he speculate that the changes can be made?

- Dr. Ernst agreed to a three-year average of collectible receivables over 120 days old. Why agree to an average based on historical data for receivables over 120 days old, but not use the same methodology for those under 120 days old? (*Note*: He may say that his suggested collections procedures may not have much effect on older receivables.)

Report/Witness Strengths

- Dr. Ernst has spent many years lecturing and explaining complicated issues in a teaching environment, and I expect that his expert testimony will reflect this experience.

- Dr. Ernst uses a research study of three radiology practices with which he is very familiar because he performed the study and produced the data. Despite our argument that these practices should not be utilized because they are not located in Nita, he may have comparison points ready and available for him to rebut why he believes the contrary.

- Our collectability rate may be seen by the court as being low at 40 percent if the court is not familiar with medical practices and the historical difficulty of collecting accounts receivable. Dr. Ernst has made a career out of increasing the profitability of practices. We may need to try to get him to admit that when he starts working with various practices on their collections, they are not at maximum collectability. He is hired as a consultant to increase profitability, and he charges a fee to do this.

Date: September 3, YR-0

Confidential Analysis by John Ernst, PhD(Lynne Allen's Valuation Expert)

Memo from John Ernst to Lynne Allen's Counsel, re Cecilia Price's Report and Potential Testimony

CONFIDENTIAL WORK PRODUCT

Issues Regarding the Report

- Ms. Price works for Dr. Allen on an ongoing basis and prepares his annual corporate practice returns. She is not a neutral witness.
- Ms. Price analyzed a three-year period of Dr. Allen's accounts receivable collections information; however, she chose to use the last year as a basis for the percentage collectable despite the fact that a three-year average would have been higher.
- Ms. Price agreed to a three-year average of the collectability of accounts receivable over 120 days. Why not average for under 120 days? She is not consistent with her methods.
- Ms. Price applies a 10 percent discount to the receivables. She applies this discount because one of Dr. Allen's employees who worked in collections resigned after date of filing. I have several problems with this:
    - Where did the 10 percent come from? How was this quantified?
    - How can the loss of 10 percent be supported? How does she know the new employee won't be better at collections than the last employee? This is very speculative.
    - If the employee was replaced with someone with less experience, aren't they being paid less than the employee who resigned? If so, why wasn't this adjustment made?
- The collection rate on receivables of 40 percent is extremely low, even if it is historical. We need to press the point that this is a low rate for this type of practice. Since Ms. Price doesn't have any other radiologists as clients, she doesn't have anything to which to compare Dr. Allen's collection rates.
- Did Ms. Price consult any studies at all? Did she look at industry data?
- Did Ms. Price utilize business valuation resource data to compare collection rates? If not, why not?
- How can she assert that she believes the practice is attempting to maximize revenues without comparing Dr. Allen's collectability with that of other medical practices?

- The fact that Ms. Price indicates that Dr. Allen is not pursuing the most aggressive collection practice because of the fear of malpractice suits contradicts her previous statement that Dr. Allen's practice is trying to maximize profits.

Report/Witness Strengths

- Ms. Price is familiar with Dr. Allen's practice.
- Ms. Price is familiar, and may have worked, with Dr. Allen's staff.
- Ms. Price is qualified in business valuation and may certainly use this as a reason that her testimony should be more credible.
- Ms. Price is experienced as an expert witness.
- The percentages of collectability calculated by Ms. Price are correct regarding what happened in Dr. Allen's practice historically over three years. However, it seems self-serving to take the third year because the data is a lower percentage of collectability and assists her client.

Date: September 15, YR-0